BREAKING
THE MOLD

BREAKING THE MOLD

BookLocker.com, Inc.
2009

BREAKING THE MOLD

By Kriston Couchey

This book is dedicated in honor of John Eugene Couchey Jr., who died at the young age of 48 in the service of the King.

TABLE OF CONTENTS

INTRODUCTION

In 2008 I awoke in the middle of the night with these words running through my head, "Take the articles you have written and put them into a book." I acknowledged this and went back to sleep only to be woken up by my wife saying out loud, "I know the name of your book! And I can see the cover!" Of course my wife had no idea the Lord told me earlier that night to write a book. So, here it is. This book is a compilation of articles from the last nine years with the things the Lord has revealed to me about His desire and purpose for the church in the days to come.

Some of these insights may challenge you, some may offend you, and some may inspire you. But in all this, please know I am convinced that it is the Lord who has given me this insight. Some of the foundational truths have been introduced to me by Father's of the faith, of whom my own earthly father was chief influence. I have the utmost honor and great respect for these.

I did not write this to validate or invalidate the ministry, gifts, or call of anyone else. That is the work of the Holy Spirit. I am called to be obedient to write what the Spirit has been teaching me. It is not the messenger who is the judge it is the Word Himself who is the standard by which all men's works will be judged. Even this book will be judged according to the Word Himself, who is the expression and container of all truth. This truth has come from the Lord teaching me by His anointing through revelation, trials, and great failure. I pray that God in His great mercy will give you a greater vision of who He is and the great inheritance in Him we have. May God open the eyes of our understanding to comprehend how great the plans and purposes He has foreordained for us who hold fast to Him.

CHAPTER ONE
A NEW DAY

I am no seer. I dream, I feel, and I hear things in the Spirit. So, when the Lord spoke to me and asked, "What do you see?" I stopped working momentarily and saw nothing. Then by faith I looked again with my spirit and I saw a golden sun rising, having already fully broken over the horizon. Immediately this scripture came to me: *...unto you that fear my name the Sun of righteousness will rise with healing in his wings...* Then the Lord spoke to me, "It is a New Day!"

We have passed a threshold in time that is ushering us into the culmination of all things. The age of the church has ended, and we have entered the age in which the Kingdom of God will be fully established on earth as it is in heaven. This book is about the transition of the ages, and changes we will see as the sun rises higher in the kingdom sky.

The religious mold of the past that has defined and confined the church has cracked. I hope through this book to break religious mindsets and further move the church on into its destiny. This destiny is our inheritance we share with Jesus Christ in the kingdom of our Father.

Since the fall of mankind, it has been God's purpose to reunite Himself with His fallen creation. God has been in the business of revealing His glory throughout the ages in order to bring about the redemption of His creation. He manifested His glory to Israel through delivering them with signs wonders and bringing them into the Promised Land. He ultimately manifest His glory through Jesus Christ; the living Word of God. He is the perfect expression of Father; the one in whom the fullness of God dwells without measure. For the last 2000 years in the church age

He manifest His glory through those whose lives have been poured out as a sacrifice unto God. These have given their all for the sake of their master and Savior Jesus Christ.

But now, in the transition of the ages, through Jesus Christ He is uniting Himself with all of His redeemed church even as a groom unites himself with His bride. The Glory of the Ages will manifest Himself fully through His beloved church as they receive the inheritance for which they were created and foreknown.

This inheritance has been reserved for His children. All of creation has groaned for this, and all who are His sons (both men and women) have groaned for this, and now we are about to see the culmination of all the ages as his children receive the inheritance for which they have groaned and persevered. This inheritance is the very essence of God in Christ imparted to His children by the Holy Spirit. As a Groom is united with his Bride, so Christ in this new day is uniting Himself in fullness with His beloved. This union will reveal the Father to mankind through His children in the same manner Jesus revealed the Father 2000 years ago.

THE CLOSING AGE

Jesus referred to the kingdom of God in terms of plants that grow, bear fruit, and are harvested. The work done by Jesus and the early apostles was that of planting and watering. The increase came from God. The seeds of the kingdom have been planted in the hearts of men and we are about to see the fruit of that labor come forth.

The closing age has been a time of growing, changing, increase, reformation, and transformation. This metamorphosis has been both painful and beneficial in the restoration process that God has initiated since the fall. The church is about to see the completion of her long hard labor in the wilderness. Truly she has been a woman in the wilderness, hidden away for a time until she brings forth her children. She has been as a tree planted and nurtured until she brings forth the fruit for which she was planted.

The mature fruit being harvested in this new day does not look like the growing plant of the last age. It looks like the first fruit, the seed that was planted in the ground and died that it might not abide alone, but bear much fruit. This New Day is the harvest resulting from that seed of the kingdom planted 2000 years ago. Jesus is that first fruit. We His brothers and sisters are the harvest of the seed that was sown in death that we might be raised to new life. The fruit He has patiently waited for is the sons of God being revealed in this unfolding age.

We have entered into the fullness of time in which we will see the harvest of all things, both the righteous and the unrighteous. We will see the maturing and reaping of the fruit of wickedness across the earth, as the sons of the devil manifest the deepest depravity of sinful man. More importantly, in the deep darkness an ever increasing light will shine. We will see a maturing and reaping of the fruit of God's righteousness as the sons of God are revealed in the kingdom of their Father.

UNVEILING THE BRIDE

In this day God is revealing sons and daughters; the brothers and sisters of Christ. While this is true, the Revelation of John paints a symbolic picture of the Bride of Christ (the church) as the New Jerusalem, the holy city and dwelling place of God. This symbolic picture gives us insight as to God's purpose and desire to be in complete union with His children. In John's revelation, the Bride has made herself ready, and has been prepared by God for an intimate consummating relationship of UNION with The Lamb, and in doing so union with the Father Himself. After 2000 years of struggle, strife, and pain, we are at the door of this consummating relationship. The bride is about to come into the fullness of the purpose for which she was called out and set apart; **Becoming ONE with God**.

The Revelation of John culminates with a picture of the New Jerusalem coming out of heaven as a bride prepared for Her Groom. This is the age of the unveiling of the bride, the New Jerusalem (the revealing or unveiling of God's sons). All of creation has waited for her appearing as the veil is lifted. All shall see the Bride seated with Christ in the heavenlies. She is being unveiled on the earth to fulfill her destiny as the God's ruling city. Her destiny is to fully establish the kingdom of God on earth as it is in heaven. Heaven and earth are becoming one.

The purpose of this union of the spiritual realm and the physical is greater than just a merging of two different realms. The full establishment of His kingdom on earth as it is in heaven will bring about the consummation of love's desire, the passion of God to reestablish forever intimate unbroken fellowship with mankind. Romance is at the heart of God's dealings with men. A bride's desire is to give pleasure to her groom and be the center of his affection and attention. It is a groom's greatest pleasure to love and please his wife. Christ yearns for his bride to be bone of His bone and flesh of His flesh; ONE body with ONE head, who is Christ, Husband of the bride.

This love affair is the centerpiece of this new day, as all that has been keeping the Lord from union with his children will be removed. Heaven and earth will both shake as the Lord brings His kingdom in fullness. Heaven and earth will be in harmony as His will is done on earth as it is in heaven.

WHAT IS BEING BUILT?
Heaven is my throne, and earth is my footstool; what house will ye build me? saith the Lord, or what is the place of my rest?
~God~

There are two cities being built on the earth. You are either of one city or the other, there is no in between. These two cities are "institutions" men look to for security and safety. God is building the New Jerusalem, the holy Bride of the Lamb. The book of John's Revelation also talks of the other great city being built called Babylon, the great harlot. These two cities are two women with two different motivations. The Bride is motivated by love for her groom. The Harlot is motivated by the desire to please herself at others expense.

Babylon is the same word in the Hebrew for Babel. Babel was the place where men built a tower for their own names sakes that resulted in God confusing men's speech and scattering them across the earth. Babylon is the world's system or structure established by the will of men that appeals to and empowers the self centered pride of men. Babylon can metaphorically be called the "confusion of men's works".

Some have considered certain nations to be Babylon as their wickedness increases. Some hold that Babylon is the system of dead religion that has left its first love and become a harlot. In fact it is all of the above. Babylon is simply this; what men build for themselves to please self. It is the world's system of operation. Any institution that sets up systemic self-centeredness in its operation becomes Babylon. Babylon is the dwelling place of demons, every unclean spirit, and the cage of every unclean and hateful bird. Its ruler is the god of this world's system; the Devil.

THE FOUR HORNS (POWERS)

Babylon is empowered by four forces or powers that affect all of humanity. These four are **military power, political power, religious power, and economic power.** These are the four powers or "Horns" (described in Zechariah 1) that have scattered and laid low God's people so they are not able to raise their heads. The pride and selfishness of men has used these "forces" to build

Babylon into a habitation of wickedness. All earthly governments and institutions are dependant upon these "forces", and are part of the system of Babylon to the measure they are used for selfish ends. They all "trade" with her and use her wickedness to advantage themselves.

THE CHURCH DEPENDANT ON THESE POWERS
The powers Babylon has used to build herself have truly laid the church low and stolen her true Identity in Christ. The church has committed the adultery of depending upon these powers as her means of security, empowerment, and sustenance instead of the Lord.

God calls His people to build up Jerusalem and leave Babylon saying, "Come out from among her that you may not share in her destruction". We are in the world but not of it, we are salt and light. To come out from among her means to stop being united with the purposes and goals of institutions that are Babylon. For the children of God, this means to come out from joining with institutions that call themselves "church" but are like the world. The church becomes the Whore of Babylon when it is self-serving and uses any of these four "powers" to advance her cause. When the church depends upon or finds its security in the ways of the world they manifest in the church as the following:

WORKS OF THE FLESH (Military power/ power of the flesh)
this manifests as dependency on works of the flesh; including control, manipulation, intimidation, flattery, activities not directed by the Spirit but men's wisdom, focus on physical structures, and organizations. This also includes allegiances to earthly governments and their agendas and wars. In summary: dead works.

DIVISIONS (Political power) this manifests as doctrinal division, hierarchies, denominations, power struggles, competing agendas, splits, sects, racial and ethnic divisions, prejudice, nationalism, etc.
RELIGION (Religious power) manifests as legalism, religious traditions, regulations, requirements, self-serving ideologies, liberalism, and conservatism. These are ideologies that are not born of Spirit revelation but men's wisdom. Religion can also result from interpreting the truth found in scripture apart from the Spirit's revelation.
LOVE OF MONEY (Economic power) this manifests as dependency on mans financial resources for security, influence, and the ability to get things accomplished. This also manifests in preferring the rich for positions of influence, equating financial success with godliness, and false teachings in giving.

ANTICHRIST SPIRIT

The meaning of the word "Antichrist" is: opposition of Christ through "replacing" or being "in the room of", "instead of", or "as" Christ. The antichrist spirit attempts to work wherever the gospel is preached in the attempt to stop the work of the Holy Spirit. The antichrist spirit tries to "replace" the manifestation of Christ in His people with any thing else birthed in men's flesh or soulish endeavors. **The fours horns of power are used by the antichrist spirit to replace the reality of Christ and His power in the church.**

The enemy doesn't just take away what we have; He offers His own false version "instead of" Christ that is pleasing to the flesh. The four powers are the "instead of Christ" or "antichrist" replacement for what we are to have in Christ. The spirit of antichrist seeks to mask itself as Christ, in place of Him and convincing those who receive what this spirit offers that they are in fact worshipping Christ Himself. This is opposition to Christ that is embedded and systemic within the majority of churches.

The Spirit of Christ does not rely upon the methods and resources of men to promote its purposes. When the control of men and their wisdom and works are rejected and cast down, then the Spirit has room to reign. We don't defeat the antichrist Spirit by attacking it or the people who move in it. We overcome through BECOMING ourselves what God has given us of His Divine Person to become. We become as He is by the Blood of the Lamb, the word of our testimony, and not loving our own lives (our own wisdom and works) unto death.

CHRIST: THE DIVINE REALITIES IN HIM

What are the spiritual realities or power that God builds the New Jerusalem with? All that He is building is found in Jesus Christ, for He is forming Christ in His sons. He is building them as a temple, a body, and a City to dwell in. Its construct is the very essence of who Christ is. The following four chapters of this book speak to the Divine realities in Christ that the spirit of antichrist has replaced with the four horns of Zechariah 1. When we walk in these Divine realities, we can clearly discern what is of the Lord and what it not. These realities are not just doctrine. They are manifestations of person of Jesus Christ, and the kingdom He is establishing already among and within his ekklesia (called out ones).

CHAPTER TWO
DIVINE AUTHORITY

Jesus Christ **right now** has all authority in heaven and on earth. God's intent is that we as His people walk in the Divine Authority Christ Jesus walked in. The power of the flesh cannot build the kingdom of God. Nor can the authority given by men. Only Divine Authority from the throne of God has the power to establish His kingdom.

The Lord spoke to me, "I have given you great authority; use it!" I was taken back by this. I said "yes Lord, but what is my authority, what do you want me to do?" He then began to reveal to me that the authority He had given me concerned the burden He had given me for His bride; her release from bondage, and preparation for union with the groom.

As time went by I saw more of the great need for deliverance of God's people and it broke me. The passion of God rose up in me for His Bride and I literally stood up and said "I don't care if I am a failure and am sinful, send me Lord; I will go!" Immediately there came upon me strength and faith that was truly HIS life flooding my being. Suddenly doors opened for ministry. The power and presence of God began to manifest as the Lord made available to me the opportunities to exercise the divine authority He had given me.

I was clothed with His strength and power through standing in the place of divine authority in Him He had called me to. In Him I found my place of authority; as by faith I went forth in confidence in His ability to work His work in me and through me.

"If ye abide in me and my words abide in you, ye shall ask what ye will, and it shall be done unto you." ~Jesus~

Divine authority to ask whatever you will and have it done is a result of abiding or being in Him. This has to do with your place in His body. We each have an anointing from the Lord that is a portion of His being. Abiding in Him is simply stepping into the place or sphere of authority we are anointed by the Lord to take.

"In my Father's house are many dwelling (ABIDING) places; if it were not so, I would have told you. I go to prepare a place for you. And if I go and prepare a place for you, I will come again and take you unto myself; that where I am, there ye may be also..."
~Jesus~

Jesus was not referring to a place we go when we die or get raptured. He was speaking to the disciples about the realm of the spirit in Him in which each one has a place and a function. That place of anointing within His body is in reality a place of Divine Authority in the heavenlies. Our abiding place in Him is our inheritance as children in His kingdom. We are the manifestation of His kingdom authority on earth; as we execute God's directives and instructions in the places of authority we have been given.

PLACES OF AUTHORITY
The Lord spoke to me in a dream and said, "Stand with and before me with confidence" I came to understand that this meant standing confidently before His presence to receive grace, but also meant confidently standing with Him in the sphere of Divine Authority He had given me.

I had an experience one summer while waiting upon the Lord. He had directed me to pray for a month at a Christian retreat center. My times of prayer became waiting on the Lord, and quieting myself in His presence. During one prayer time I had an experience in which I became "enlarged" and my being filled up the spiritual space around me. This "enlargement" happened twice that summer. It also happened while praying in another region I was sent to preach.

I wondered about this, and the Lord showed me that I was given Divine authority in these locations. And truly, in both of these places I exercised His Divine authority to preach, teach, and confront false authority. He used this experience as a sign to me to show me the spheres of authority He had given me to "occupy".

We literally spiritually "occupy" the sphere of authority we have been given. We "become" authority in these places. In a parable Jesus spoke, a nobleman gave treasure to his servants and said, "Occupy until I come". This word "occupy" means to do business. Use what you have been given to possess and make it profitable for the kingdom. Take the places the enemy has stolen and make them places of the presence and power of God. Do God's business in your sphere of authority. As of now, there are malignant principalities and powers that inhabit the heavenlies. They must be cast down and their places occupied by the children of God in order to establish fully His kingdom on earth.

Occupying or doing God's business in the heavenly realm isn't simply a matter of shouting or ranting at the devil in warfare. It is established through rest, confidence, and victory in the inward life. This denies and disarms the work of the devil. The Lord directs us to assert the authority we have already been given in various ways when we reach a level of faith able to confront strongholds in our places of occupation. This may include praise, dancing, decreeing, etc. These activities are subject to the Holy Spirit's direction and not just a formula for spiritual warfare.

Victory is maintained through standing in rest in the place given by Him. Rest is the ultimate state of faith in which we disarm all the enemies that have been or are trying to occupy (do the business of the devil in) the sphere of authority we are given to occupy. It is yielding total control to God in confidence and faith. Rest takes our hands off of trying to fix the situation ourselves. It is waiting on God to give direction and empowerment to accomplish His will in what He has entrusted to us.

The enemy's strategy is to get us out of rest (fullness of faith). Being in fear, doubt, anger, or any sin, gives an open door for the enemy to work in our sphere(s) of authority. As we rest, we become confident enough to ignore the devil. Our Divine Authority naturally dismantles the works (business) of the devil in our sphere. In reality the battle is not about doing, but BEING!

The battle really is within ones self. Once authority is exerted within; it requires nothing but faith and obedience to enforce it in our sphere of occupation. In each area of an individual's life where there is defeat, the place of occupation they are assigned also experiences the same defeat. In the same manner, when victory is secured, and confidence and authority are reinforced, so the place of occupation experiences the same measure of freedom.

The church has allowed sin to take dominion because we haven't spiritually overcome and exercised our Divine authority to open and shut doors in the places we are given to occupy. To "occupy till He comes" is to do the work of opening and closing doors in our sphere of authority. We open doors to the works of the Spirit, and close them to the works of the devil. We are each given keys to the kingdom in our places of authority.

"And I will give unto thee the keys of the kingdom of the heavens, and whatever thou shalt bind on the earth shall be bound in the heavens, and whatever thou shalt loose on the earth shall be loosed in the heaven." ~ Jesus~

Jesus has all authority in heaven and on the earth. He gives men portions of His kingdom to rule and reign (occupy). This authority can either cause great harm, or great benefit. All believers are gatekeepers with the sole keys to their spheres of authority be it a location, ministry, or gifts. You become a gatekeeper in your sphere as you allow or disallow things, forgive or not forgive sin. It is an eternal authority given, and is a great responsibility to those who will learn to walk in it.

The church has opened the doors for the world, the flesh, and the devil to overcome and defeat the church and those it is sent to deliver. It is time to stop blaming the world for being what they are, and get our own house in order and start being what we are.

"...and having a readiness to avenge all disobedience, when your obedience is fulfilled." ~Paul~

Meaning: when the church comes into complete obedience to the Lord it is in a position to bring judgment on the world for its disobedience. Occupying a place of authority in Christ in obedience naturally brings judgment on sin, and releases the power and presence of God.

Many would fight the battle of good and evil in the flesh; mobilizing Christians with all the powers of the four horns to accomplish what they believe is God's will. This is not a battle won by warring in the flesh; it is a spiritual battle, speaking forth what God is actively speaking with divine authority. The divine authority of God's children must be established in the heavenly places before the realm of the earthly authority comes into obedience to God's will.

AUTHORITY EXPRESSING DIVINE LOVE
And Jesus went forth and saw a great multitude and was moved with compassion toward them, and he healed their sick.

In Jesus we see Divine Love that moved Him to exercise His divine authority. The compassion of God preceded many great miracles Jesus performed.

Matt. 9:36 Jesus had compassion on the people and sends out the disciples with authority to cast out devils and heal the sick.
Matt 14:14 Jesus had compassion and heals the sick
Matt. 15:32 Jesus had compassion and feeds the multitudes.
Matt 20:34 Jesus has compassion and heals two blind men.
Mark 1:41 Jesus has compassion and heals the leper.
Luke 7:13 Jesus has compassion and raises the widows son from the dead.
John 11:35 Jesus weeps and then raises Lazarus

While not every miracle Jesus did has compassion recorded as preceding it, in Jesus we see Divine Love of God moving him to perform the miraculous works of God. He didn't work wonders with Divine Authority to just prove He was the Son of God, he did the works of God to express the Love God has for people.

In the kingdom, God's children express His Divine Love through Divine authority in the same manner that Jesus did. We also are called to be ONE with Father's heart of Divine Love like Jesus. He is not calling us to perform works to prove we are His sons; He calls us to His LOVE that meets the needs of the broken around us, just like Jesus did. It is not by works the world will know we are His, but by Love that expresses itself though good works. It is not works we aspire to, it is becoming ONE with the Lord's heart that we aspire to. As we abide in His Love, so also He has prepared works for us. We no longer do what we do for any motive other than the Love of God in our hearts that compels us.

The Kingdom of God was manifest when Jesus exercised Divine Authority out of love. Paul wrote essentially that the kingdom is not words, but power. The kingdom of God is love expressed through power to deliver, heal, change, and restore. Jesus didn't come to just be a nice guy; He came to destroy the works of the Devil and redeem mankind through the work of the cross, the greatest expression of love ever shown. Jesus said, *"...as my Father has sent me, even so send I you!"* We are the containers of His Love, expressing this love through the authority He has given us to do what Jesus did and more.... Truly the kingdom of God is come in His people.

DIVINE AUTHORITY WITHOUT DIVINE LOVE

It is possible to train disciples, speak forth the mysteries of God, and perform miracles and healings, and all the while not partake of the Divine Love of God. I would challenge you that much of the Divine Authority expressed in the church age has been done apart from the motivation of His Love.
Jesus said it like this:
Many will say to me in that day, Lord, Lord, have we not prophesied in thy name? and in thy name have cast out devils? and in thy name done many wonderful works? And then I will profess unto them, I never knew you; depart from me, ye that work iniquity. (Lawlessness).

Jesus is telling these who have exerted Divine Authority in effect: You did not partake of my nature, and become acquainted with Me. Doing His works apart from His heart is considered iniquity.

Jesus' disciples did not fully understand the Divine Love of God until after the impartation of the Holy Spirit at Pentecost. James and John wanted to call fire from heaven and consume the Samaritans. Jesus rebuked them saying, "You do not know what manner (nature) of spirit you are of." Paul speaks of Divine Authority (exercising gifts, miracles, etc) expressed without love.

In fact, I Corinthians was a letter to a church familiar with exercising gifts but lacking in love.

People throughout church history have exercised authority and gifts; all the while partaking in godless activities and attitudes. But they still exercised their God given Divine Authority. The lack of God's nature within left a gaping hole in their places of occupation for the enemy to come in and bring destruction and confusion. We see it exhibited every time a scandal rocks the church and men and women fall.

THE ANOINTING

We are anointed like Christ. Jesus was the Christ (meaning=anointed one). When the Lord anoints with His Spirit He gives both the Divine Nature (love) of God and the Divine Authority of God. The Divine Nature we are anointed with is the manifestation of Christ IN us. It is nurtured through learning to walk by faith (rest) and obedience to the indwelling Holy Spirit. Truly learning to rest with Him IN us is the key to embracing His nature. We are changed as we behold Him as in a mirror, within our innermost being (Christ in me).

On the other hand, Divine Authority is the place IN Him we are called to walk. Abiding IN Him is where we bear much fruit. There can only be true full rest IN Him when His Resting place IN us is established first. We rest "under the shadow of His wings" when these two aspects of UNION with God are present in our lives.

David and Saul are examples of two people anointed by the Lord who took different paths with that anointing. David was an example of a man after God's own heart. The Divine Love of God found a resting place in the heart of David; manifesting the character of God. David spent years shepherding, fleeing in the wilderness, and hiding in the cave of obscurity. David was tested and brought forth like purified gold. In the end he came to occupy the place of authority prepared for Him by the Lord.

Samuel anointed Saul as king and scripture says"... *God gave him another heart...*" Saul had available to him in the anointing of the Spirit the Divine Nature AND Divine Authority of God. In His anointing, God had made available to both Saul and David all they needed to be king; both character and authority. Saul did not nurture the nature of God in his heart. Instead he chose the approval and opinion of men over the approval and opinion of God. The Lord doesn't anoint people with authority without the character to use it wisely.

THE ANOINTING TEACHES YOU

David was taught by the anointing and became a man who embodied God's heart. He exercised the authority of that anointing with God's heart.

But the anointing which ye have received of him <u>abides in you,</u> and ye do not need that anyone teach you; but as the same anointing teaches you of all things and is truth, and is no lie; and even as it has taught you, <u>abide ye in him</u>. ~John~

Men **choose** to exercise the authority of the anointing, while not letting the anointing teach them to walk in the character/nature of God. God lets men use Divine Authority they are given and does not take it away. Truly the gifts are without repentance.

I was anointed years ago for what I am beginning to do now. I saw the power and authority of God released years ago while I was still in bondage to many "sins", yet "leading" others. But that anointing has been teaching me, sometimes very painfully. The authority of the anointing DOES NOT GO AWAY even if we practice sin. This is how men have excused their weaknesses and failures and have continued to live double lives. This is a snare that all of us in the church must beware of. Men have assumed that exercising Divine Authority was God's approval of them. There is nothing farther from the truth. God did not approve of Saul. David recognized the authority of Saul's anointing and would not harm him. And yet, David would not wear Saul's armor or submit to Saul's abusive ways.

DIVINE LOVE WITHOUT DIVINE AUTHORITY

It is no coincidence that the early monastic movement gained momentum in the western church as Divine Authority of the common believer in the church was usurped and replaced with the false authority structure of the Roman church. When Church of Rome declared its "preeminent" authority and demanded the submission of all the regional churches, a dead system of religion then gained control and dictated "church law" to people.

Since there was no other "Church" to be a part of, those wanting real relationship with God were limited to pursuing only the divine nature of God. Many dedicated themselves to meditation and prayer. The exercise of Divine Authority to establish God's kingdom outside the walls of the monastery or desert cave generally ceased. Even the authority to be forgiven was now in the hands of clergy.

This monastic pursuit of the divine nature of God still goes on today. It goes on in many church groups whose emphasis is brokenness, humility, the fruit of the Spirit, and character building. These are "wilderness" ministries. These are necessary ministries that prepare the hearts of people to walk in Divine Authority.

THE WAY OF THE WILDERNESS

The church on the most part has been in the wilderness since the demise of the early church's Divine Authority. This is the place Moses, Elijah, David, John the Baptist, Jesus, and Paul were all trained and tested before going forth in authority. In this wilderness, God teaches us to know Him, His heart, and His ways. The heart issues dealt with in the wilderness are necessary to receive character changing impartations of God's Divine Nature. It is a place of solitude and realization of ones own weakness. But it is also the place where we recognize God's strength that overcomes our weaknesses.

Sometimes unbelief can grow in the wilderness that keeps people there and they never leave. They have seen their weak flesh and don't trust it. They think, "How could God use a worm like me and give me authority to accomplish mighty things for Him?" Some never get beyond seeing their own weakness to embracing God's strength in order to take the Promised Land of divine empowerment. We can see our sin and live in an unhealthy guilt and fear of God that never recognizes and embraces His goodness and grace that gives strength in our weakness. Truly knowing we are desperate sinners is not the same as knowing intimately the one who has saved us from them. One of the lessons of the wilderness is to know our desperate depravity. But a more important lesson is learning to know the God who loves us and delivers us from that depravity. For those who have learned the lessons of brokenness, embraced the love of The Lord, and nurtured His indwelling nature within; the day has come for the Kingdom (Divine Authority) of God to be fully manifest.

WALKING IN DIVINE AUTHORITY
"I am not worthy that thou should come under my roof; but speak the word only, and my servant shall be healed. For I also am a man under authority... ~Anonymous Centurion~

The centurion understood true authority and its function. His understanding unlocked great faith that much of the church has missed for 2000 years. When we are commissioned to carry out a task in our place of occupation (sphere of authority), we can obey the Lord without doubt that His will is going to be accomplished. The centurion simply had to "say the word", and by the authority granted him by the Roman Emperor it was as good as done. He was in his proper place of occupation (business). Exercising our authority is done with confidence and rest when we know our place of authority. We then KNOW we have a right to exercise authority in that sphere. This is great faith, knowing our place of occupation, and exercising the authority we are given in it.

When the Lord told me to write a book I had no doubt that I had both the ability and authority to write it. Like the centurion, if you are doing what you do with the Divine Authority of your master, then you need only to exercise that Divine Authority and it will accomplish that for which it was given. The working of God's Spirit wanes and waxes in expression through God's children to the degree to which they are exercising Divine Authority in the spheres they occupy. To the degree we function fully in our place of Divine Authority is the degree with which God can manifest his Glory in that place.

You can only occupy that which is given by the Lord and no more. Presumption of authority in a sphere can open the door to the devil, bring you under great deception, get you a good whooping, or even cost you your life.

WHAT IS MY DIVINE AUTHORITY?
"As the man who, taking a far journey, left his house and <u>gave his estate to his servants and to each one his responsibility and commanded the porter to watch</u>." ~Jesus~

Most sincere believers at this time do not walk in the basic levels of authority that every believer has been given. This common believer authority is over sin, sickness, the devil, their families, and possessions. When we begin to move into broader realms of Divine Authority, the majority of believers who are sincerely seeking the Lord are ignorant about their Divine authority. Some of the authority in gifts and ministry include: miracles, healing, prophesy, deliverance, preaching, teaching etc. Some of the spheres or places of authority include regional areas from work places, congregations, city blocks, nations, and the whole earth. Everyone is given a portion, and not all portions are the same. These portions are closely related to the burden and heart for others the Lord has given you.

So, why do few walk in divine authority? God's people lack understanding of what divine authority is, and the place of authority God has given them personally. Much of the divine authority of the believer has been "surrendered" to a religious system that relegates or abdicates the exercise of divine authority to a few. Often those few who learn to exercise Divine Authority are raised up into positions of leadership. Like Moses, people expect leaders to hear God for them and follow the leader instead of the Lord. Many have freely abdicated their Divine authority to a "church" system, a doctrinal understanding, or leader.

A great many walking in Divine Authority are not equipping others to enter in their own places of authority. Instead, a codependent (mutual need) relationship develops where people find their security and needs met in the leader, and the leader gets their sense of worth from people needing them. In this situation, people become dependant upon leadership for instruction, direction, revelation and "positions" of authority (which is not spiritual in nature, but works of the flesh). Leadership becomes dependant upon people for income, position, worth, and fulfilling their need to be needed. Being spiritually dependant upon another person bypasses the true authority a person is given and makes it ineffective. The following is an example from my own life.

SPIRITUAL DEPENDENCY

I was asked by a friend to come to a weekend Christian gathering she and her husband were hosting. I was not a speaker at the meetings, but the Lord gave me a word for it. I felt Sunday would be the day to go to this meeting to honor the hosts who were to speak that day. As the weekend approached, there was a conflict that came up for that Sunday. But I kept my peace in God, and was confident He would work things out.

Friday, I called a local pastor for some information and the conflict was resolved. I mentioned the meetings, and that I wasn't sure if I was going Saturday or Sunday. He asked to pray with me for clarity. I didn't feel any need for him to pray, but he was being nice, so I said, "Yes", and he prayed. It was a generic prayer that asked God to give clarity and direction. I thanked him and hung up.

Saturday, my sense of God's presence was gone. I tried to rest in God but He was nowhere to be found. I felt as if I had tunnel vision and was in a spiritual stupor. All day as I went about business I sought God for clarity and direction but the unction and fire of God was missing. The day passed and I didn't go to the meetings because I had no unction to do so. I decided to go Sunday since the day had gone by and I found no peace.

I got up Sunday to the same thing. On the two hour journey I began to fight for my rest in God. I was unable to find it and became frustrated, wondering what was wrong. The thought then came to me that the problem was the pastor's prayer. I prayed, breaking off and rejecting the prayer said over me. Suddenly peace and rest from the presence of God overtook me, and the literal feeling of tunnel vision left as my spiritual perception returned. I went to the meetings, was blessed greatly, and was asked to give the word, which I had told no one I had.

The Lord revealed to me over the next few days what had happened. It was not witchcraft from the pastor. It was not demonic oppression trying to keep me from giving a word. God was not mad at me or withholding Himself from me. It was a simple principle called dependency. I had accepted a prayer for me for something I already had established in my life; the guidance of the Holy Spirit. In effect I had turned from the guidance of the inner peace and rest of the Lord in my own spirit to receive what a man had to offer in its place. I cut the cord with the Lord and handed it to a man.

I experienced a very similar experience when the Lord told me to go to the wilderness and quit all ministry work. The very next day I quit all ministry work. Most importantly I came out from the inappropriate subjection to a leader. That dependency tie being severed was like a fresh breeze from heaven. The level of revelation and vision I received after that was like waking from a dream.

BABIES ARE DEPENDENT, NOT ADULTS

When I was a baby I was dependent upon others to teach me, feed me, protect me, and correct my mistakes. This training is so that I might learn how to become a full functioning human being. It is appropriate for a baby in Christ to get teaching and direction from the mature (elders) as to how to hear and walk by the Spirit. A prayer for clarity might be appropriate for a new believer who has not learned to "hear" the voice of the Spirit. But when a baby grows up and learns how to fend for itself and goes off to college, it does not need to be diapered, hand fed, and put to bed on time. In the church, when believers learn to hear and know the instruction and voice of the Lord for themselves they don't need someone to do it for them anymore.

Many in Leadership do not know how to release people to this type of maturity. This is due to lack of understanding what REAL authority and leadership are called to be within the church. This is hard for the current church leadership to accept, but the reality is that the church in its current state is in general NOT walking in its Divine Authority because of this dependency. The church is full of dependant believers that should be walking in the guidance and authority of the Holy Spirit but don't know how. The subject of leadership will be brought up later. I will finish this portion on dependency with this: Spiritual Dependency robs men and women of their Divine Authority.

AUTHORITY AND GIFTS

Divine authority to exercise a "gift" and the gift itself are inseparable. In other words, you cannot exercise a gift apart from the authority from the Lord to exercise that gift.

Jesus said: " The Spirit of the Lord is upon me because he has anointed me to preach the gospel to the poor; he has sent me to heal the brokenhearted, to proclaim liberty to the captives and recovery of sight to the blind, to set at liberty those that are broken... "

Jesus was anointed to preach, proclaim, and release, and heal. He was anointed by the Spirit with abilities (gifts) to carry out His mission. The gifts were for the sake of exercising His Divine Authority. If I have the gift of healing, then I have also been given authority to exercise that gift. The centurion understood completely that the healing of the servant had everything to do with the authority and ability (gift) given to Christ to heal. Gifts are tools to accomplish the will of God. They are the vehicle to express Divine authority. If someone is exercising a gift then there is an authority of God to do so. God always gives grace (the ability to accomplish) when He gives authority.

AUTHORITY OVER OTHERS

...The kings of the Gentiles exercise lordship over them, and those that exercise authority upon them are called well-doers. But ye

*shall not be so, but he that is greatest among you, let him be as
the younger; and he that is prince, as he that doth serve. For who
is greater, he that sits at the table or he that serves? Is it not he
that sits at the table? But I am among you as he that serves.*
~Jesus~

It is clear from Jesus that we are not called to exercise
authority upon or over another as the world exercises authority.
This worldly authority is called hierarchal authority. That type of
worldly authority is **NOT** the Divine Authority God establishes
His kingdom with. Yet much of the church confuses and mixes the
understanding of divine authority with the world's hierarchal
authority.

We are given authority to free others from bondage, bring
them to maturity, and bring them into accountability and
submission the Lord. This is *being as the younger* and *as he that
doth serve.*

CITIZENS OF HEAVEN
*"But now they desire a better country, that is, a heavenly one;
therefore, God is not ashamed to be called their God, for he has
prepared for them a city."*

When the fullness of God's kingdom is established on the
earth the rule of law will become obsolete. The establishing of true
righteousness undermines the need for government laws to exist.
As it is now, governments are needed to enforce law. But, law
enforcement is only needed when people are lawbreakers. There
is NO law or need for it for those who walk by the Spirit; for by
nature (God's Nature) they fulfill the law and need not be
conscious of any law to please God.

Earthly government laws and power are powerless compared
to the power of the righteousness, joy, and peace that are the

expressions of the kingdom. Yet unrighteous men in earthly governments and unrighteous law are a cause for depression and fear for many who claim the name of Jesus. Many Christians regularly eat of the tree of the knowledge of good and evil by trying to change earthly governments and laws with the arm of the flesh. When God's people are busy trying to control earthly governments by legislating wickedness out of existence, wickedness GROWS. For law incites people of lawless heart to sin. The external enforcement of law has served a limited purpose for a season, but does nothing to establish the Kingdom of God. Those who have entered the Kingdom have all authority in heaven AND earth unrelated to men's governments. You cannot enter this kingdom through law, but by becoming like a child.

It's time to teach people how to live By the Spirit with the law of God IN their hearts. When we do this, there would be no need of external government. THERE WILL BE NO NEED FOR RELIGIOUS OR GOVERNMENT LAWS OR RULES SOME DAY. No one will say "know the Lord" for they all will know Him least to greatest, and His laws will be in their hearts.

My kingdom is not of this world; if my kingdom were of this world, then my servants would fight... ~Jesus~

The Kingdom of God is a state of being. It is: Righteousness, Joy, and Peace IN the Holy Spirit. These three states of being are unreachable by external activities of men, but found only in union with God. Religion is: Seeking after God who is separate and distanced from us through the striving of works and law. The Kingdom is: God with us, in us, and us in Him. It is important first to recognize that God has given each believer the means to establish His righteous kingdom in their hearts apart from observing the law, through childlike faith. Secondly, it is important to establish the kingdom across the earth in the same manner it was established in our heart, through childlike faith that releases righteousness, joy, and peace in the Holy Spirit.

The kingdom of God has none of the foundations of the worlds systems, yet has complete authority and preeminence over these insignificant things. Jesus said, "If I do what I do by the finger of God then the kingdom of God has come." Take His work as the best example of the kingdom coming. When by the authority of the Spirit I drive a spirit of hate out of a man and he is flooded with God's love and delivered, He now needs no law against murder. This is the kingdom. It is beyond comprehension for us at this time what the kingdom coming in its fullness is like.

BACK TO THE GARDEN

We are moving back to conditions of the Garden of Eden. They were not conscious of sin as we have been. We will have come to a higher level of existence after having once known the depths of sin and been redeemed and overcome. Adam and Eve did not need to overcome the world, the flesh, and the Devil in the garden in order to live at ONE with God and commune with Him daily.

We will rule and reign as a result of overcoming to take our place in His kingdom. We have had to choose Him; a greater call, a greater Glory. There are realities of sinless perfection that are the same for both us and Adam and Eve. The innocence of not relating to God by Law will be a freedom that brings righteousness, joy, and peace. But the most important aspect of the coming kingdom is great LOVE.

A PARALLEL TO PONDER
A short story By Kriston Couchey

These men had had enough. Lifestyles and laws opposed to the commandments of God were threatening to change the very culture of their nation forever. Something must be done. So this group of concerned men fought against the tide of wickedness until they had once again made the establishing of the commandments of God honored rather than ignored or looked down upon.

The people looked to these men for direction and leadership concerning spiritual issues. They fasted and prayed. They stressed purity and strove to obey all the commandments of God and did not associate with anyone who promoted sinful behaviors or pagan religions that did not honor God. They wanted the nation to turn back to God, as it was when God first established it.

There was a nation across the sea that was taxing them heavily. These taxes were used for war campaigns and building projects in others regions of the empire. There was no representation of the people being taxed in the use of these funds. Those collecting taxes could not be trusted. There were regional governors appointed by the empire that the people had no say about. They lived opulent lifestyles that were an affront to the rest of the people in the nation. The armed troops could do just about anything they wanted and would demand things of the people and they had to obey.

These men of integrity wanted to throw off the oppressors. They wanted a nation that was free to worship God as He demanded and was built upon the foundation of the commandments. They were waiting for the right moment to once again restore their nation to its former glory and right standing as a nation chosen by God. They wanted to break free of the oppression and rise up again as righteous people who would lead the world in the light of truth; God's truth found in the scriptures.

These men were waiting for the Christ to come and restore Israel to its former Glory. But something happened they did not expect. A carpenter came along preaching," Repent! For the Kingdom of Heaven is at hand!" He did not preach about the need for Roman oppression to end. He did not join with the Pharisees (our men of integrity) in opposition to unfair taxation. He did not talk about restoring the nation (Israel) established by God to its former glory. His only interest was the kingdom of God, which was established in the hearts of men.

This man did not go to their schools. He was not of their sect. He didn't fast like them, pray like them, and he was not impressed with their abilities to keep the commandments. He spent his time and efforts with the hated tax collectors and with the people the Pharisees tried so hard to not associate with. He talked of love and the kingdom of heaven in the hearts of men that starts as a mustard seed and grows to overshadow everything else. These men wanted no part of that kingdom, they wanted their own kingdom back and he was leading all the people away from them and their dreams to restore Israel. The people talked about how unlike the Pharisees he was. Yet the Pharisees would have to lay down their goals, ideas, and dreams to follow this man. That was out of the question. They loved their nation. God had established it and made a covenant with its people. They believed this man was fighting God by not joining with them.

The worst of it was he claimed God as His father, making himself out to be equal with God. If God were his father then he would have the interests of the nation on his agenda. The last straw was when he came to Jerusalem and the people hailed him as the king. He offended the business community that was making money in the temple by calling them thieves. Then he had to audacity to tell the people to "give to Caesar what belongs to Caesar and to God what belongs to God." He may as well promote the empire fully with that heretical statement. **"He must die so the nation will be preserved"**, was the determination of the chief priest. The scribes, Pharisees, and elders decided to go down a path that was dark indeed. The rest is History.

DREAM: ALLEGIANCE TO THE FLAG

I had a dream in which I was in a room with many Christians. They were standing in rows forming two columns pledging allegiance to the Flag of the United States of America. I was stirred in my spirit immediately that this was wrong. I decided not to say anything as I was afraid of what people would think. But then the power and fire of God rose up within my being so powerfully that I knew it would be disobedience if I kept silent.

I walked to the front of the people and said by the Spirit, "This nation is not under God, and it does not have justice for all, you are pledging your allegiance to lies!" There was stunned silence in the crowd, as the meaning of what I had just said began to sink in to the people. I then awoke.

EARTHLY GOVERNMENTS WILL END

The Lord clearly spoke to me one day that the Bride became a harlot when the church embraced the sword of Constantine. This man's conquering **in the sign of the cross** was one of the most critical blows to Christianity that it has received in history. From this point on, the Spirit of anti-Christ had full systemic entry into the hearts of those who claimed the name of Christ. This is not about just the Roman Church; it is all who place their dependency, security or allegiance to any force, nation or institution that uses the means of the flesh to accomplish its goals, even goals that are said to be God's goals.

Constantine had a mandate as an earthly government ruler to bear the sword. He did not have the authorization of God to establish the church with it. The mandate of earthly governments to bear the sword will end as this Kingdom Age advances. We will see the disintegration of men's systems as foretold by Daniel. The "Stone not made by hands" in Daniel 2:44, is the Kingdom of God which crushes ALL nations of the earth to dust and is established as the only kingdom. Let's be found in His kingdom and not in allegiance to the kingdoms of men.

No man that wars entangles himself with the affairs of this life, that he may please him who has chosen him to be a soldier.
~Paul~

CHAPTER THREE
DIVINE UNITY

Communion, community, common unity: these terms describe what those led by the Spirit have in common; **UNITY**. This communion (common union) is not based upon a church affiliation, doctrine, leader, or location. It is based upon: *"... the unity of the Spirit in the bond of peace."* Complete unity with God is our destination in the kingdom. The kingdom will be released fully in those who learn to walk in union with the Holy Spirit regarding the heart and purposes of God. Not just obeying Him, but coming into agreement with His judgments and heart. The Bride of Christ is in complete agreement with the passion and purpose of God's heart toward creation.

In this new day of the kingdom advancement we will see the progressive union of God with His children as He purges the earth of its rebellion and pride. As a groom consummates his love for his bride; so the Lord is consummating a union with His people that will express the very essence of God's divine nature.

When those who walk with God in union enter fellowship, worship, and mutually encourage one another; you will see an even Greater Glory. This is an outpouring through those who have gathered unto Him as His body. Each one has first individually learned to walk in union with the king as the head, and then in communion with their brothers and sisters.

... and the Lord, whom ye seek, shall suddenly come to his temple, and the angel (messenger) of the covenant, whom ye desire: behold, he comes, said the LORD of the hosts.

God is fitting together a temple made of living stones that is at this present time scattered and coming out of wilderness trials and purification. But they are coming together in this time of earth's upheaval and turbulence as a wave of refreshing to the earth. God is dwelling in His glory in these, and their common union is that they are partakers of His Spirit in nature and authority. They have learned to be at rest with God IN them and they IN Him. They have learned submission and accountability to God, and have come to maturity seen in obedience out of love.

COMMUNION IN COVENANT

There is coming a power and glory pouring forth from those walking in the "common unity" of the Spirit in the One Covenant of The Blood of Jesus. Truly this is the Wedding Covenant of Union with Christ. If you are led by the Spirit, you are His child, and are already in a completed covenant of unity with everyone else in heaven and earth who is one with God. In the One Covenant of "Common union" with God and each other, power will be released so mightily that many people will move beyond their old alliances and allegiances to their own church "communities", denominations, leaders, and organizations.

The communion of the saints will be seen in the broader sense in its reality; as what God has deemed in "union" with Him is blessed, and that which is not in union with Him will not endure. You will know those in union with Him by His heart, His presence, and His power expressed in those He chooses to glorify; for we are the Glory He now chooses to clothe Himself in. He is the Glory we are clothed in. The new day's work of God is going to be characterized by one thing: LOVE. By this ALL men shall know we are His disciples. The body will fully express what the Head (Jesus Christ) has created it to express; the divine nature of God seen in the person of Jesus Christ. God is pouring out a baptism of His Love and goodness to bring unity of purpose, heart, and vision to His people in this new day.

We receive fullness of vision individually, when we corporately enter into relationships with each other based on His Love and Intimacy. Where there is no real Love relationship, focus is placed on gifts and titles. This has turned "church" into wrangling over gifts, titles, and power. In this setting, vision is dimmed and splintered. Each sees their own vision as the whole. Vision will be whole only in communion (Common Union) with God, and with the saints. This gives us grace to receive from one another. In this union of His Love, all receive their vision from the Lord as to what it is HE desires to build, and how He wants each to build it.

JOINING IN UNITY

There is only one source of true unity for gatherings: the Holy Spirit joining together those He chooses to unite. We are all one in the Spirit as the Body of Christ. But, we are all to connect in the place where God has designed us to connect. It is possible to unite with people and form groups that are not connected by the Spirit's joining, but men's doing. Two things give witness that the Holy Spirit is uniting people in connection. The first is a deep abiding peace of the presence of God in our innermost being. The second and most important is love expressed one to another. Paul writes that we should **"....guard the unity of the Spirit in the bond of peace."** In other words, the unity of the Spirit is something that can be lost if not guarded.

CHURCH STRUCTURE

In 1994 I had my first experience meeting with a group of people outside the institutional church. In this unorganized small group I experienced the power and work of the Spirit in a way I have never experienced before. In 2001 we finally left the institutional church at the command of the Lord. We fellowship and worship with others in unstructured settings that many today label "organic" or "simple" expressions of the body. But, God is not limited to a small gathering or a large gathering, He does what He wills. Jesus modeled many styles of ministry; in the temple, in synagogues, in homes, in large crowds and small. He simply did what his father was doing at the time as He was led by the Spirit. He lambasted the Pharisees who were full of methods and laws that made them "successful".

When Jesus left His disciples he didn't give them a blueprint or instructions on church structure. He gave them one command: To LOVE ONE ANOTHER as He had loved them. He told them that Loving God and Others was the fulfillment of the law. I tell you that this kind of love is also the fulfillment of the church. All new "Structures", will be judged by their ability to express Love efficiently and in a way that does not give great cause for questioning motives or intent. Many will not be able to flow in the new day simply due to their inability to operate in a structure whose mortar is Love. The lack of love causes men to try to keep structures together with control.

I've observed a friend try to write down and redesign a new structure the church should take, and he ended up in frustration. How do you redesign and restructure a family? A family that is already built on the Love of Father expressed through the Son. Its structure has not changed just because someone else has come in and redesigned it as a network, a dictatorship, a democracy, or a business.

CHURCH IS FAMILY

Church is family. In a family, the father is the head, and the older siblings are given authority to watch or help their immature brothers and sisters until they are mature enough to care for themselves. In turn, those who were once young and needed help have now become mature. They are now old enough to watch over (oversee) others in until they are mature as well. But, a father has the ultimate authority in a family.

In my own family, I have the authority to tell my eldest daughter, "Don't let the younger ones go on the road!" Because of her maturity and wisdom that exceeds her siblings, I trust her to take seriously my command to protect her brothers and sister. I will also tell the others "listen to your sister." They also know implied in that command to them that my eldest only has a level (boundary) of authority that pertains to their protection. If she was to get bossy and start acting in a manner that was not in accordance with her mandate to watch and protect, the other kids would know and say, "You can't tell me what to do".

I might also tell one boy, "Help your older brother with the dishes". This implies that the one being helped is in charge of doing dishes and the younger helper **for that time period** is to assist in the dish washing. Because it is the job of the elder, he is responsible for the task and takes the lead, but I also expect they will both work together come to an understanding on how to accomplish the task. The older better not take this opportunity to boss his brother in that task, for I would reprimand him for this. I would encourage them to share responsibilities and take turns at different jobs so they both can be proficient at the job.

I might ask my older daughter to help her younger brother tie his shoes, and in the process show him how it is done. Any harshness by the daughter or instructions beyond my will for this endeavor is inappropriate and will receive my correction. My desire for my children is similar to God's for His children. I don't want one to be following and subject to the other all of their days. I want all to be individuals who enter into full maturity and take control of their own destinies without being in bondage to the will of another.

THE CHURCH AS A PLAY FORT

I liken church to the building of a fort by an elder son. He is oldest and has more vision and wisdom. Because of this, the others will naturally follow his lead in this endeavor. But, what happens is that now it becomes his fort and he exerts his authority as the leader. This causes great consternation when the others don't do it the WAY he desires it to be done. He will correct and direct them according to his own wishes. They will play along with this game for a while as it is fun to have a club that has some sort of purpose to their playful imaginations. He appoints other leaders, be they princes, queens or helpers.

The fantasy is fun for a while. But after a while the others get bored having no input or say as the direction of play. A fight breaks out and one or more leaves to build their own fort so they can be their own kings or leaders. Finally, it is time to come home for real, and the fantasy leaders and followers' status disappears under the house of their father who holds real authority in their lives. So it shall be in the church.

TRUE KINGDOM AGE LEADERSHIP

There truly is a leadership in the church that leads and serves. But, "leaders" can act as if they have ALL the fullness individually that people need, when in reality "leaders" (ascension gifted individuals) have specific roles with a specific task to accomplish. Elders are those recognized as mature and stable; they oversee, counsel, protect, and teach. Mature ascension gifted individuals are elders as well, but they are not the head, Jesus is.

Leaders don't direct gatherings; they give heed to the direction of the Spirit, even His work through the immature. If leaders would learn to simply "Be quiet" and stand as watchman overseeing when the Spirit is not moving or speaking through them, they might just be surprised at the levels of gifts and authority God has placed in His people. This makes the Holy Spirit the Lord, and we are just watchmen as overseers.

True leadership is all about seeing Christ formed in people and manifest through them. Christ is the "head" as the body corporately functions and expresses Him consistently through the various members of the body. This does not negate the job of elders to oversee, nurture, correct, and protect the flock. It will be the goal of leaders in this new day to see themselves decrease, and Christ increase in presence, power, and diverseness of expression through the body. The day of the one man show is over. Leaders must be laying down their lives for the sheep; their ministry, their gifts, their pride, in order to see the body come into completion in Christ.

There is going to be great diminishing of the positions of men in the church for those that would receive the fullness of what God is doing in this new day. This diminishing is simply the Lord placing things in the order He intended it. Yet the exercise of Divine Authority of all God's children is going to go ballistic. Divine authority is not about the submission of men to other men; it is about walking in the realm of the Spirit in faith.

DIOTROPHES = TODAY'S MODEL LEADER
I wrote unto the church, but Diotrephes, who <u>loves to have the preeminence among them</u>, did not receive us. Therefore, if I come, I will cause his deeds to be understood, speaking against us with malicious words, and not content with this, he does not receive the brethren and forbids those that desire to receive them and casts them out of the church... ...Everyone gives testimony of Demetrius, even the truth itself; and we also bear witness, and ye have known that our witness is true. ~John~

When reading these verses from 3rd John, we have to ask the question: who is in charge of this congregation? Is Diotrephes? If he is, then John tells Gaius to not follow him by saying: "...*do not follow that which is evil, but that which is good.*" But If Diotrephes is not the leader, then who is? Is Demetrius? If so, why is Demetrius not rebuking and casting out Diotrephes with his pastoral authority? The lines of authority are not matching up with today's model of church leadership. Would an apostle today tell a congregation to not follow their leader? Why are leadership roles so ambiguous in this scripture? It's because the church did not have pastors as head of the church, they had a plurality of eldership (mature believers) under the headship of Jesus Christ.

The problem that John had with Diotrephes he would have with the current model of church leadership. In many ways leadership has usurped the "Preeminent" headship role of Christ in the church. This type of leadership has become systemically entrenched and accepted as God ordained in most sectors of the church. This false leadership structure comes from the hierarchal Roman church. It is the use of fleshly political power that is nothing more than a manifestation of the spirit of antichrist. Antichrist meaning: **instead of Christ or in the place of Christ**.

It is the antichrist spirit that has set up an abomination in a wing of the temple (the church). While this spirit may one day manifest in the world as one evil world leader; the antichrist spirit seduces the church to give fealty to something "instead of" Christ. The antichrist spirit opposes every manifestation of Christ come in the flesh; that flesh being "**Christ in you** the hope of glory."

How better to do it than to "replace" the head of a church (Christ) with a false head. Leaders taking the place as the "Head" disconnect people from Christ and His manifestation through His people. The antichrist spirit has used good men and women to oppose Christ through cutting off the expression of Christ in His people. In this new day it will not be tolerated.

Prevalent in existing church structures is the existence of truly gifted and divinely authorized vessels whose boundaries of authority have been stretched beyond their spheres, becoming inappropriate and stifling to the work of the Spirit. It is important to recognize "boundaries" of leadership. The apostles were definitely leaders, but within certain boundaries. Within congregations and regions you must have leadership. The appropriate boundaries of leadership must be learned and observed in order to maintain an atmosphere of liberty in the Spirit. God's desire is that everyone be able to freely express the portion of Christ each one is given. At this time in history there is very few who do not go out of bounds in their leadership roles. Systemic ignorance has defined leadership roles in the church up to this day.

There are individuals with an anointing to lead (spearhead / go before). But, how is that authority expressed? Even the expression of true divine authority can be done in assumption, presumption, and tradition, and not based upon the Spirit's desire. The gift of apostle and prophet are the foundational gifts which recognize, encourage, and quicken other gifts to find their place and function in the body. But apostles and prophets have boundaries that limit them in a congregation. Apostles and prophets must be building a foundation of Christ for others to build upon. It is the job of apostles and prophets to see Christ formed within the body. Paul's letters to the churches was to tear down the false that had come in (antichrist), and rebuild Christ.

Equipping is a progressive process of Christ revealing Himself in individuals and congregations, and is not a stagnant process. You know when a group has lost the leadership of the Holy Spirit when they are teaching the same things over and over. There should be progressive revelation brought forward by those gifted to train and release people into maturity in Christ. If we are subject to the headship of Christ and submitted to the leadership of the Holy Spirit, then God will make available the gifts we need to train us up.

Real church leadership establishes, restores, builds, and then gets OUT OF THE WAY so that those following behind can pass. Many spiritual leaders get to the end of their anointing and mandate for a group of people and their "followers" can go no further because they are in the way. The maturing person stuck in the system can get hungry and bored. The problem is not the hungry and bored; it is the false leadership mindset that has killed the work of the Spirit. Better for that equipper to let those who are trained move on to their destinies ALONGSIDE AND EYE TO EYE WITH THEM, and find more immature to teach what they don't know.

There was a time my wife and I received much insight and teaching from a man that taught about dreams, visions, and hearing God. That foundational teaching of hearing God has been a basis for our spiritual lives. He is truly a leader, has led us into these truths, and still has the anointing to lead. But his heart is to see others walk in this revelation and not depend upon him. We relate on an EYE TO EYE basis with friendship and mutually submitting and receiving one another.

There is a non-hierarchal pattern of leadership. In its simplest form, someone goes before in a realm of spiritual life and teaches others to enter that realm as well. But that does not make them a perpetual leader of that person. One day they will grow up and become mature themselves. Paul had specific things he did, plant, move on, restrengthen, plant, move on, and restrengthen. There were others gifts needed to come in and impart their portion within the boundaries of their authority. Scripture says Apostles are first, prophets next, then teachers, etc. This is not necessarily a hierarchal order, this is the plurality of gifts "order" to establish foundations and train a congregation. In the book to the Hebrews they were rebuked for not becoming teachers. This was because somewhere along the line there was a breakdown in the building process. Someone built with wood, hay or stubble, and the writer had to go back and tear down the false doctrines and restrengthen the true foundation of Christ.

In a congregation of 100 people we ought to see 20 or 30 mature elders able to freely teach, train and preach at a high level of discernment and revelation. Maturity is an individual embracing and manifesting consistently both the divine nature and authority of God. It is wonderful to see the Spirit and Life released by mature and immature vessels that are given place to exercise the gifts and show forth fruit of the Spirit within the body.

SEASON OF MATURING THROUGH EQUIPPING AND TRAINING

There is a season of training and maturing when God puts people in your life to help you grow. Elders teach the younger, but even that has an end as a younger becomes an elder. The mandate of the mature (elders) to protect, train and care for the immature and weak was never intended to be for the perpetual subjection of people. There are boundaries of authority, and authority to equip given for seasons. A teacher has authority to teach and train a child, but you would think it odd if a child after 20 years still was learning their multiplication tables.

It is no different spiritually than it is in the natural. I train my children and teach them to do what is right as a child. When they grow up, they go out from under my authority to raise them. They no longer need my permission or censoring of their activities. A father would never continue to subject his grown child to themselves, but rather, they rejoice in the maturity and grace of a child weaned and raised to stand on their own two feet; a mature adult like themselves. A father may have wisdom and warning for them if he sees them in danger or going in a path that is wrong, but he is no longer the authority that disciplines and directs them.

I have personally submitted to the authority of others to teach and train me for a season, but when the Lord spoke to me and said, "You are coming of age!" it would be inappropriate for me to go back and feed off people that fed and cared for me as an immature believer. I can now feed myself as the anointing within me teaches me. And yet I can still learn from both the older and the younger as the Spirit moves upon each.

UNITY THROUGH MUTUAL SUBMISSION

Receiving and submitting to the gifts on another's life is essential to walking humbly before God and men. Fully embracing this revelation will set things in order in the body quickly.

Testimony: I was given an invitation to minister internationally and was ready to go, except for one thing. My wife had misgivings about it. I felt in this she was just too reluctant and cautious, this was MY ministry trip and my opportunity to exercise a new anointing and the Lord had given me. The Lord then spoke to me: "Listen to your wife and submit to her in this". WHAT? I am the spiritual authority of the household and this is my ministry! "Be in unity with her." Wow! , I repented and did as I was told. I had a talk with my wife that changed everything: how I see ministry and my role in my family.

I determined to be in unity with her in everything we do. That does not mean she runs things. It means I will not do anything that she has a lack of peace of the Holy Spirit about; money, ministry, etc. We are now moving forward in unity, with small times of readjustment. It is a check for me as my wife has much more discernment than I on many things. She herself is submitted to me and seeks my approval on things, though I trust her enough I usually say, "Dear, if you feel you should do it I trust you, go ahead." We have mutually submitted to one another.

The Lord showed me that our relationship is a picture of divine authority in the body that submits to and honors one another's place and gifts. In the same way we will see unity in the body as leadership submits to the gifts and voice of the Spirit in others, and looses its need to rule and dominate the people they have been entrusted with.

SPIRITUAL FREEDOM

When the Lord prompted me to start a home prayer group last year I did not have a clue as to what the Lord was doing. But now I understand more of His purpose in this. While I share many things with these, there have been revelations in this prayer group through others whose revelational gifts surpass mine. I have at times sat back as a "watchman" as God moves. By the Spirit at times I step forward to "establish" or confirm something.

A seer in the group is my 12 year old. Her visions are accurate and timely. There is the young man who gets specific words of knowledge and visions. That would be my 9 year old. My 11 year old gets dreams, interprets visions and has a heart of mercy and to pray for the sick. My 6 year old has made statements, such as, 'God says "No more watching bad movies".' We meet with a couple whose gift is encouragement. The husband is an exhorter with a prophetic seer gift and the heart of the father's love.

All of these are free to exercise their gifts and anointing as the Spirit leads. My greatest joy is to see them develop in the freedom and grace of God in the calls and gifts on their life. Congregations miss God because they have cut off the voice of the Spirit in the people of God and made them slaves to fulfill their own vision. If you are an equipping leader, here is your vision: **Teach others to do what you do and make room for them to do what they do and be who they are.**

CORRECTION

I truly believe in a God ordained structure in which all equippers and elders are in mutual submission and accountable to one another. God has **not** set up a hierarchal pyramid of church leadership of inferior's submitting to superiors. Those that are mature are expected by the Lord to deal with error and sin with uncompromising truth in love. It is the call of elders to rule in this way. A corrective word to a person or congregation by the Spirit from ANYONE will bring judgment if not heeded. Correction is the Lord's correction. He has told me when I have corrected someone strongly, "if you do what this person is doing I will correct you TOO!!" We cannot assume because the Lord gives us a corrective word that now we are in a place of authority "over" that particular person or group. This is not true, and is a dangerous thing to assume.

Correction does not put others under our authority; it puts people in a position to be accountable to God. If they refuse it, they will pay the consequences from His hand not ours. Jesus even said, "I do not judge you, my words judge you." If a person so chooses for a season to be subject to the judgment of another ministry or person for restoration after falling into sin; then by ALL means let the restoration begin. But, let those restoring do it in a spirit of meekness and gentleness. Many see sin in the camp and run for structure and law to stop it. The answer is not to bind people under the authority of others or law, the answer is speaking the truth in love; correcting in all humility.

RESTORATION OF THE CHURCH

The Lord has placed on my heart an analogy I believe reflects His plan for the restoration of His church. The analogy is one of a Hotel built in the old west during the age of the horse and carriage.

Initially the character and structure of the building reflect the age in which the hotel is placed in service. Over time, the original character and structure are barely recognizable as fads and styles from different eras are tacked on, until its "tackiness" makes the hotel obsolete for modern use. It is also unrecognizable as being from the age for which it was built. Finally, the hotel is unprofitable and is ready to be torn down in order to make room for a building that can function prosperously in its place.

The owner makes a decision to "restore" the hotel to the original character and structure of the old west. He begins by determining what is "age" appropriate and removes all portions of the building that do not express the "character" of that "age". Some foundations were added to the original structure with later additions. These additions are torn down, and the foundations are broken up and removed. The original foundation is once again the sole support for this structure.

There were walls and rooms added within the structure making smaller divisions of the original openness of the lobby and "common room". These walls are removed and the openness is returned. The original hotel rooms were later divided into two or three smaller rooms. The purpose for the division was for selfish gain. These dividing walls are removed and the large rooms are once again opened. The windows, doors, handles, lights, trim, window treatments, and decorative designs must all be replaced with pieces that reflect only the age for which the building was built.

Once the restoration is complete, the hotel is now reopened for business, and a revival of hotel life and traffic flourishes because of the beauty of the restored edifice.

There is an "age" to which the temple of God is being restored. The "Kingdom Age" appropriate "character" traits that reflect the kingdom of God will again be seen in the structure of His house. Restoring this character and structure is the first priority of the Lord. He has brought refreshing to strengthen us for the task of restoring His temple (people). But, true kingdom life awaits the restoration of the habitation God desires to indwell.

MINISTRY CHANGES

In Jesus' day He confronted, offended and threatened the religious mind and system. So also in this day true kingdom ministry will confront, offend and threaten the "system" of church life today. This genuine kingdom ministry will affect every aspect of what some would call the equipping or ascension gifts; apostles, prophets, teachers, pastors, and evangelists. These changes will be born out of a love and humility that has a clear vision of the heart and purposes of the Lord. Those willing to walk in this Love and humility will be willing to change the manner in which they operate in order to serve the body in a manner pleasing to the Lord.

While all equipping ministries will see great change, apostles and pastors are the two that are going to change the most dramatically. This is because of the distorted understanding of their function and purpose in the body. People are expecting them to be what they are not called to be, and do what they are not called to do.

MINISTRY OF THE APOSTLE

There are currently many different spheres of unbiblical apostolic ministry. Today's apostle can be equaled to a president of an organization. On a larger scale the apostle has a multitude of churches under their authority. High visibility Apostles today relate to those who are willing to cut a covenant with them by either signing a contract or agreeing to covenant with them which makes them "part" of the network of apostolic leadership.

There can be also a monetary agreement of payment for being part of the network. They function financially like denominations in many ways, except the focus is on apostles as sole leaders, not the corporate administrative oversight like denominations. Some apostles on local levels serve the role of traditional pastors. Their network is the people who are under them and they may be in covenant with them by membership or tithe.

The role of apostle is going to change most dramatically because of true revelation on the ministry of apostle that has not been manifest yet. Walking the way of the crucified life will transform apostolic understanding greatly. An apostolic understanding of laying down your life for the sheep and being a true servant of the bride will break the chains of the unbiblical "covering" doctrine, denominationalism, and many current overbearing networks. This will release the Spirit to cross-pollinate what men have boxed and limited. A release of regions to complete freedom and reliance upon the Spirit will be the result of conviction and repentance over the way in which the Lord's church has become the possession of men.

There will be access across the body for various emphasis and realities given to apostles to flow freely everywhere. Regional leadership will be the strength of the church as multiple regional elders oversee the church of a city or region. Elders are the mature. Apostles, prophets and other gifted individuals are also Elders when they have matured. Elders may be gifted as any of the ascension gifts or they may not. There will be only ONE church in a region with many gatherings. When a whole area is in the kingdom, there is no need for covenants with scattered groups of diverse doctrine or structure. All who make Christ Lord are in the Kingdom.

Some Apostles will be mandated to establish and build in cities and areas. Some will be more body wide or message oriented, establishing foundations in the broader body. Many will do all of the above. People will gather in more organic expressions. This means gathering in small groups to fellowship, pray, and minister to individuals. This serves a purpose, but there will also be larger gatherings that train and equip. While fellowship will be more intimate and open in small gatherings, under the headship of the Lord regions will gather corporately. Both expressions will serve a purpose. The larger meetings will be for training, teaching, and corporate praise and worship. The smaller meeting will focus on body ministry and for doing the work of the ministry.

Locally there will be a premium on hearing the Lord for yourself and not looking to the pastor, prophet or apostle for direction. Apostles will fight for the freedom of the body to express the mind and heart of the Lord corporately. Gatherings will be more worship and Spirit led corporate preaching, prophesying, and teaching rather than the organized structures of man controlled order. Apostles, prophets and pastors will serve alongside other mature individuals (elders) as facilitators and watchmen rather than the sole sources of inspiration and teaching. You may not even know who an apostle is in a typical meeting as the Lord will simply have His way. Apostles will relate as friends and equals, not solely as "teachers" or censures. Team leadership and corporate body ministry will be the heart of apostles. Their greatest joys will be to see others step out boldly in ministry gifts and calls, even to their own decrease. They will be firm with those who desire is to draw men unto themselves. They will see clearly wolves whose intent is to devour or divide the sheep and deal swiftly with them.

While apostles have a vision of structure in order to build, they do not focus on building a structure. They want to see Christ established and built in the hearts of men and women. They are concerned with not letting structure get in the way of the Holy Spirit manifesting Christ in His people. This is true apostolic ministry.

A teacher's main task is to define and disseminate the pure doctrine of Christ (principles). Prophets impart unction and vision of the "Christ Life" to people personally and corporately. Apostles are focused on seeing the "Christ Life" activated in people personally and corporately. They also function as a teacher or a prophet in order to accomplish this. Prophets impart, apostles activate. Impartation is the seed; activation is the bearing of fruit.

Apostles lay foundations of the knowledge and reality of Christ, explain it in doctrinal (understandable) terms, apply it through the prophetic word, and activate it through **opening the spiritual door** for (releasing) people to their spheres of occupation. While they could do all this by themselves if needed, team ministry is the way in which apostles will prefer to function, gathering people with these various gifts and abilities in order to establish more effectively what they could not do by themselves. They will humbly recognize and release members of the team to function in unity in order for a greater manifestation of Christ and His power.

APOSTOLIC MANDATE

God is **purpose** focused and not **position** focused as it pertains to His people. In other words, position is trumped by purpose. It is God's purpose to see his Son formed in the lives of each believer. It is the mandate of God's apostles and prophets to fulfill this purpose, that Christ may be formed in his fullness of stature IN His people. The mandate is fulfilled through going before and making a way for others to walk in the measure in which each apostle has received. For an apostle, that means activating and teaching people to find rest in the presence and nature of God, as well as enabling people to express His authority in the same manner in which the apostle functions.

God is raising an apostolic people, not an apostolic hierarchy. This is a people who know how to rule and reign with Christ.

They have overcome the world, the flesh, and the devil in their spheres of authority and occupy the place in the realm of the spirit prepared for them by the Lord. This is about purpose. I become concerned when position becomes the focus, because it happens when purpose is not being implemented and other things have cooled the love of the body.

Structures and appropriate ministry connections exist and have their place. But, these are not the center of God's attention. Becoming one with His people is His center of attention. Jesus longs to express His heart for people to the church, and then through the church to all the earth. This is the REALITY we are looking for in "church", and the heart of true apostles.

APOSTOLIC AUTHORITY

Apostolic authority is "atmospheric" in nature. In other words, apostles have the ability in ministry situations to know the mind of the Spirit as he moves through those in a gathering and speak the will of the Lord and enable it to be accomplished. As overseers they have an "overview/oversight" of what the Spirit's intentions are. Apostles carry an authority that enables or quickens others to their own anointing. You could call it a sphere of authority that is corporate in nature, while not being hierarchal. If someone claims apostleship but is not bringing forth the gifts in others they are not an apostle.

Jesus told Peter that whatever he bound on earth is bound in heaven, and what he loosed on earth is loosed in heaven. Apostles also have authority in the realm of the spirit to open and shut, bind and loose spiritually. Where many prophets are intercessors, Apostles become intercession in that they have the immediate presence and power of God in their divine place to release and activate the work of God ON earth as it is in heaven, the kingdom of heaven come to earth.

APOSTOLIC RELEASE

It is solely the Lord who releases (promotes) people to a place of overseeing or equipping work in the body of Christ. Jesus is the one that gives direction to lay hands on and release people to ministry or eldership. It IS NOT the decision of apostles as to who is ready to be "promoted" by the Lord. It took prayer and fasting for the prophets and teachers to discern **the Holy Spirit's choice** of Paul and Barnabas to apostolic team ministry. **Do not lay hands on too hastily**, because it is easy to allow man's estimation of a person's gifts and abilities to cloud the view of what the Lord sees as valuable in His sight. Fast and pray over these decisions to get God's choice and lose your fleshly perspective. Even godly Samuel had the wrong estimation of man by outward appearance.

The laying on of hands or releasing to equipping or overseeing work is not from a position of authority over the one being commissioned. It is simply inviting someone to be your co-laborer in saving, feeding, protecting, and discipling the immature. Elders and equippers relate horizontally and eye to eye, submitting to and receiving correction from each other in brotherly (and sisterly) love. There are governmental functions that give certain individuals a measure of authority to speak a decisive word from the Lord **in their sphere of burden and authority,** and these must be honored, but this has nothing to do with being under anyone else's authority.

APOSTOLIC FATHERING

There truly is a reality of fathering people in the faith. Paul had an intimate relationship with the Corinthians. He deposited his spiritual DNA in them, a relationship that only he had with them. He was first to come and birth the things of the Spirit in their midst. He loved them as a father loves their children, and they in turn must have had a special place in their hearts for him as a child does for their father.

In the natural, people or animals imprint a specific person or animal as their parent. This can happen between species. For instance, a cat can raise goats and have the goats follow and imitate it as if they were cats. You become a father to someone when you have had the first "imprint". Many want to father children they have not had a hand in bringing into the kingdom. My natural and spiritual father was the same person. I have received an impartation or imprinting of his spiritual DNA; a burden for the body of Christ.

There are spiritual orphans in the church. God sets the *"solitary in homes"*. He gives fathers to the fatherless. But it is God who determines the relationship needs and "sets" the parent with the child (metaphorically) for a season of nurturing. Some have been nurtured and come of age, and no longer need fathering. Yet, some are still subjected to apostolic fathering doctrines and practices that are hindering the maturity they need to walk in. This happens because men are following doctrinal practices and not the direction of the Spirit in their administration of their authority. It must be a work of the Holy Spirit to bring fathering to those specifically needing it.

While there is much truth to fathering, some of the apostolic fathering fad today is assuming a fathering role where there is no relational or Holy Spirit guided right to assume that role. The issue of authority and leadership based upon submission to apostolic fathering has established a false structure that has become controlling and restrictive to the Holy Spirit. Apostles must lead people into relationship with their real Father in heaven, while truly fathering those they are given to father in such a way as to not draw the focus and attention to themselves. Many "apostolic fathers" are drawing others to themselves and not the Lord. This is a perversion of an element of truth that has been made a focal point of discipleship. Any doctrine (Principle) that has become the focal point other than Christ has usurped His place.

WHEN TRUE APOSTLES COME

When true apostles come they will be desired because they are friends and not apostles. The tie that binds them to people will be love and friendship, not position and place.

When true apostles come they will be greatly gifted. They will be known for Love that is greater than their gifts. This greater love will so outweigh their abilities that those who know them after the Spirit will not seek to exploit their gifts.

When true apostles come they will prefer to listen and not speak, They will prefer not to preach, teach, and give their point of view, but will rejoice in what impartation and revelation they can receive from the various members of the body.

When true apostles come some of the greatest signs and wonders done among the people will be subtle, and won't be noticed fully until after they have left and people notice the change that has taken place.

When true apostles come the greatest signs and wonders will flow out of what seems to be the most foolish and bumbling activities they engage in. Some of these signs and wonders will be seen in the midst of what some would think are secular activities or conversation, the spiritual man will receive it while the religious mind will scorn.

When true apostles come our increase of understanding their function and place in the body will be like looking back at pictures we drew in kindergarten of stick men, and then looking in the mirror and seeing a living breathing reflection. We will say, the real thing is much better than the childish depictions we made years ago, but we did as well as we could with what we knew.

When true apostles come they will dance like children.

When true apostles come they will prefer to sit with that needy person who is annoying and ignored because they are strange.

When true apostles come you will say, "I saw Jesus more clearly than I have ever seen Him in a person before."

MINISTRY OF THE PASTOR

Today's ministry of Pastor is one of CEO and religious service director. Salaried and employed by the people, the pastor is responsible to feed the sheep. This feeding is not done by simply leading them to green pastures and still water where they can graze and drink. But today the pastor is the hand that harvests and hand feeds the sheep.

The true gift of pastor as spoken of in Eph. 4:11 is not a hierarchal role of chief executive that many groups practice. A true pastor is a nurturing, healing, caregiver of individuals or small gatherings. We call anyone who oversees a church in a "headship" role a pastor. Many called "pastor" are some other ascension gift, or in some cases, have no real gift to equip the body but are just are good communicators.

True pastors relate on a more intimate level as a loving friend whose concern for individuals will be shown by personal love and edification. They may not be recognizable as a "pastor" in a group setting at times. They will have the ability to feed people by directing them to "feed" or graze from the green pastures of corporate body ministry, and to drink peacefully from the Holy Spirit's water of Life. Pastors will have a place at times for corporate speaking; but then again, all of the body will have a place to do this. The true gift of pastor needs to find its proper place in the body. Many pastors have pure hearts and motives to serve people, but like the Israelites wanting a king, people place them in roles they are not meant to take.

THE ONE COVENANT IS SUFFICIENT

If the one covenant of Love given in Jesus is not enough for a group of people to work together in unity, will making another one of our own do any better? There is the bond of Peace in the Spirit. There is also a bond of "covenant" That men make with each other that is an agreement out of a need to "secure" relationships.

In I Sam. 20:14-17 Jonathan loved David like His own soul, but Jonathan made a "Covenant" with David out of **fear** of David changing his position toward him when he was in power. Fear has no place in the kingdom. Jacob and Laben made a covenant out of dislike to keep each other away. Covenants were made when one or more parties were unsure of the trustworthiness of the other. It is called a bond or "binding". It is a need for security or surety that causes men to make extra-biblical covenants that bind together. Where is our security? Not in the bindings of church memberships or covenant relationships, it is in the Lord alone. Jesus told us to not swear (make a covenant) at all, but to let our yes be yes and our no be no. Anything more then that is of the evil one.

When two agree on something it is technically covenant. Agreement is a required component of the Body. But that agreement is in the Holy Spirit, who gives us unity in the Spirit that is a "bond" (binding) of peace. Intentionally making a "binding" covenant not based on the Spirit's "bond" as basis for relationship turns what should be a love relationship into law. People cut covenants to keep people or relationships secure, when all we need to really do is give people to Him for safekeeping in the first place.

If we need to make a covenant to keep a group of people loving each other and sticking together, then Christ's love is not enough. It is better to live in the one Covenant of selfless Love; the one made by Christ's shed blood. His blood is sufficient and His covenant is too. It is all one sided with the Lord. He cut the covenant with us because we were the untrustworthy party who had unbelief or doubts. God cut covenant to get rid of that unbelief and doubt in Him. Any covenant other than Christ's is a division that separates us; it is an added covenant that devalues the ability and worth of the one covenant of His blood to bind us ALL with cords that cannot be broken.

There is a depth of brotherhood and love in the Spirit when He is in control and moving in power. In this setting, the constructs of men are meaningless. When the Spirit of God is moving in power, memberships, hierarchies, and institutional divisions become insignificant. This has been true of all powerful moves of the Holy Spirit. There is a unity in the Spirit that binds people together across all barriers and this is the NORMAL state of the church. We must learn to know one another by the Spirit in these days as the Lord will be rapidly moving ministries to many places to equip in a fashion that NO church denomination, apostolic network, or covenanted ministry can orchestrate. If we only trust the bonds of our membership, network, denomination, or covenant group we will miss God's messengers. The old ways of binding and uniting people will keep people sectarian and stunted.

When church government is a plurality of leadership that recognizes the across the spectrum need for cross pollination of the body, we will see great glory released to the body. This can only be fully realized when we start seeing ALL are in ONE covenant together. Many are in need of being brought the reality of the completeness and unity of covenant all His children already have in Christ.

COVERING EACH OTHER IN COVENANT

In the Body of Christ we are covered as we come into agreement with the Holy Spirit and then with others who have also come into agreement with the Holy Spirit. This covering comes from communion (common union) in the covenant that ALREADY EXISTS in Christ. When Christ manifests in His body, those who are in agreement with the Holy Spirit in prayer, word and worship become a covering for each other as they partake of the one covenant in submission to one another. As Christ is released in edification, encouragement, and even correction; we protect and care for each other in the Love of God. This has NOTHING to do with a leader, and is an ever broadening and widening reality that will be fully manifest body wide in the Kingdom Age.

You will not find the modern church concept of coverings ANYWHERE in scripture. The covering doctrine has given to men what ONLY belongs to God; our unquestioning, unwavering submission and contrition. It took me years to break free of the guilt and fear that comes from the "covering" doctrine. It is fear that keeps people bound to this false doctrine. Being part of the covering or "under authority" teaching does not mean you are evil. But, adherence to this doctrine systemically gives place in the body for someone other than the Lord to control, dictate, and take the place of "head".

The covering doctrine is about being connected to leadership INSTEAD OF Christ. Many use "Covering" as a means of keeping people submitted to their doctrines, agendas, or leadership without question. For those unfortunate enough to have come under this influence, to disagree with your "covering", or hear something from God they don't agree with is to be unsubmitted to God and vulnerable to the devil. I have good news for you, it is not true. You have no need that any man teaches you, (definitely not me) but the anointing within you teaches you. He will teach you things men may not agree with. Go with the Holy Spirit and not the "covering". Trust the anointing He has put in you by His

Spirit. This is a work of the Spirit that makes available to people all of the teaching, direction or correction we need.

When the Lord told me I was to marry the woman who is now my wife, this is what He spoke: "She will be a covering for you". Wow, what a shock of a statement. But it has been truer than I could have ever imagined. She does not exercise authority over me. She has great influence on me and sways my heart with love; just as the Bride sways the heart of the Groom. But when her prayers open a path in blizzard (seen even on radar) for us go to a place of ministry, I must say, "she is a covering for me". I cannot imagine the impact of her prayers for me. My mother is also a covering for me with her prayers. She doesn't exercise authority over me to bring me into submission to her agendas, doctrines, and church structure. But she certainly can speak to me the word of the Lord, and I must submit to the word if it is Him. I must submit to the voice of the Spirit in anyone speaking by Him, even my own children.

CHAPTER FOUR
DIVINE WISDOM

Principles are what I refer to as doctrine. Principles originate from men, devils, or the Spirit of God. There are principles or "truths" that are immutable, but even these truths in the hands of self seeking men can kill. I have done this too many times myself. We do not seek doctrine to find God; we find pure doctrine from having found God. It is ever important to know one thing: Truth IS a person. And all things done are done as an expression of Him and His judgments. You cannot judge properly anything apart from having come to union with the Lord and His heart on any matter. Doctrine is not the focus. Doctrine is words used to describe in natural terms the unchanging realities in the realm of the spirit found in Christ.

Our focus is to know Him and have Him living in and through us. When He expresses Himself in us we begin to understand and express all aspects of truth. Pure doctrine flows from a teachable spirit that is receptive to the Divine Wisdom of the Holy Spirit and what He teaches. Each person is given the anointing of God's Spirit as a means of teaching us to express the particular portion of God's nature and authority we have been entrusted with as an inheritance. The resulting truth and reality of Christ that manifests is in part expressed as doctrine.

FALSE DOCTRINE

False doctrines come first and foremost from a failure to truly know God and His character. Misconception of God is the seed of false doctrine. If you think Jesus Christ (Truth) is something He is not, all of your conclusions and beliefs reflect your false image. False doctrine is an expression of something other than Christ

(Antichrist). We should not focus on doctrine or tearing it down. We should focus on what it is in the Lord's nature and authority that needs establishing that destroys or repudiates the lies that bind and make ineffective His church.

The nature of Christ is in part expressed through words and ideas that transmit the principles of the reality of Christ. In preaching Christ, we tear down misguided doctrines. In tearing down there is great resistance from people who cling to their false realities even when faced with the presence and power of God. When doctrine flows from the reality of Christ by the Holy Spirit it has the power to change people's minds.

The way to combat false doctrine is to become the expression of Christ that confirms the principles/doctrines of Christ with the power of the Holy Spirit. The kingdom isn't just words, but power. God gives power to demonstrate or confirm His Word. This is about having the truth you are given to teach demonstrated by the Spirit with signs and wonders. This is how Paul operated. This is how we should operate: the Holy Spirit giving testimony to the Truth with signs and wonders. When there is falseness being taught there is a lack of power, and sometimes false signs and wonders.

Even genuine doctrine learned as "wrote" from others becomes distorted and used for selfish ends when the Spirit is not releasing it as His teaching, or in the time frame He desires. True doctrine not brought by the Spirit does not have the power. When we do what God is doing, and speak and release by the Spirit when He directs, there is power.

God is setting into place elders to protect and care for the flock to remove wolves who come in with seducing doctrines. It's not about control, it's about love. Out of love, the apostles continually dismissed error and exposed sin which was a threat to the church.

SCRIPTURE
The Holy Spirit inspired scriptures have three main purposes.

#1 Scripture is a testament or <u>witness</u> to the truth of who Jesus is.
Search the scriptures, for in them ye think ye have eternal life; and they are those who <u>testify</u> of me. And ye will not come to me, that ye might have life. ~Jesus~

Scripture is the measure or "witness" by which we judge what is proclaimed to be "truth". It points to Jesus and leads to the knowledge of Him. He is the fulfillment and source of its truth.

#2 Scripture is profitable for <u>training</u> in all righteousness.
All scripture is given by inspiration of God and is <u>profitable for doctrine, for reproof, for correction, for instruction in righteousness,</u> that the man of God may be perfect, thoroughly furnished unto all good works. ~Paul~

Scripture is a tool for training. By means of the Holy Spirit's Wisdom we are taught by the anointing as He brings to light the truth of the person of Jesus in scripture.

#3 Scripture gives <u>examples</u> of righteousness and unrighteousness. *Take, my brethren, the prophets, who have spoken in the name of the Lord, for an <u>example</u> of suffering affliction, and of patience.*

Let us therefore make haste to enter into that rest, lest anyone fall after the same <u>example</u> of disobedience.

There is a common phrase that goes like this, "too much Word (scripture) you dry up, too much Spirit you blow up." It is not a matter of too much scripture or too much Spirit being out of balance. You cannot have too much of the Holy Spirit who is the ONLY one that brings you that which is from Jesus the Living Word Himself. The use of this phrase comes from a lack of understanding the nature of the scriptures, and the nature of the Holy Spirit. Which is more important; The Holy Spirit who is God or the Scriptures which are a witness (testament) to who He is?

Reading about Abraham Lincoln does not make you his friend and confidant. The tool used to help make you more like Jesus Christ is not more important than Christ. You can have too much of a focus on the Scripture and use it's truth apart from Christ Himself. Many today use the scriptures like the Pharisees, they think in them they have life, but haven't continually found life in Him.

LOGOS = THE WORD

The LOGOS is referred to by John as Jesus Himself, the Divine Wisdom of God. The meaning given is: **the living voice of logic.** The definition of the word LOGOS does not refer to scripture. The verbal expressions of the Word (Jesus) or Divine Wisdom are recorded in scripture; But the Bible is only empty words apart from the Divine Wisdom Himself speaking His living voice through it.

John the Baptist was a witness (testimony), but the one testified about was more important than the one who testified. The Word Himself far surpasses a book. Recognizing that the term Logos in scripture is referring to Jesus and not the written text does not belittle the inspired scriptures, but glorifies Jesus. The place of scripture needs to be balanced, and used as it was intended. The Lord speaks and works mightily through the written scriptures as He breathes on it to teach, testify and correct by use of example.

The Lord Himself speaks WITHIN our inner most being. We cannot ignore Him who speaks from heaven (where we now dwell always seated with Him). We are His dwelling place, we hear Him speak from this dwelling and obey the "Living Word", and become the "Living Word" ourselves as we are in union with the Lord in heart, purpose, and deed. Our own words becoming a Sword that separates.

A QUESTION

Is it possible to walk fully in union and obedience to the Lord without knowing any scripture? YES! Adam, Enoch, Noah, Abraham, Isaac and Jacob did not have all the scripture to study, but had relationship and a place with the Lord. We can be grateful we have much more knowledge and clear testimony in the Scriptures.

The problem with the church is not lack of knowledge of scripture; it is lack of knowledge of God. The Lord dismantled my performance based mindset about reading scripture. He did it by speaking something to my spirit and then later showing me the scripture that testified to it. Scripture reading and study is good. It becomes dead religion when you measure your spiritual maturity or righteousness by your reading habits.

KNOWLEDGE OR HIM?

I heard a youth group leader say to the youth, "It is important to know what you believe or you could fall away when you go to college." In my spirit I replied, "No, it is important to know WHO you believe." That is the difference between knowledge of scripture and an intimate knowledge of the Lord. We can pursue knowledge of principles and truths, or a love relationship that uses scripture to get to know Jesus. Paul said, "Let the word of Christ dwell richly in you." This is not scripture dwelling me, but HIM the WORD dwelling in me with all wisdom and understanding. Scripture is the measure we use to judge what others proclaim as being the WORD in them. It is a testimony, an example, and profitable for training in all righteousness; but the Word in you is Christ in you. The experience of visions, dreams, impressions, intuitions, divine insight, revelation, and unction of the Holy Spirit is the WORD in you bringing you the divine wisdom and understanding of the mind of the Christ.

SPIRITUAL DISCERNMENT-
MAKING RIGHTEOUS JUDGMENTS
But he that is spiritual discerns all things, yet he is discerned by no one. For who has known the understanding (mind) of the Lord? Who has instructed him? But we have the understanding (mind) of Christ. ~Paul~

Having the mind of Christ is the possessing the Divine Wisdom of God. It is the Word made flesh in you. Having correct discernment is simply seeing things with the mind of Christ. Paul was a spiritual man and put on the mind of Christ and was able to judge things as the Lord judges them. That is why he could write scripture. He was not writing from his own perspective, but out of the perspective that gave him the ability to judge all things rightly, the mind of Christ. All believers can have the mind of Christ working in them. One day no one will say "Know the Lord", as ALL will know Him.

For those that are according to the flesh know (have in mind) the things that are of the flesh; but those that are according to the Spirit, (have in mind) the things that are of the Spirit. ~Paul~

Discernment is the ability to discern or distinguish what is of God and what isn't. The lack of spiritual discernment is a result of walking after the carnal or fleshly mindset. Many spirit filled Christians practice a spiritual discernment on par with the "pre-Pentecost" Peter. Peter accepted Jesus, walked on water, had breakthrough revelation, saw Elijah and Moses, healed the sick, and cast out devils all before Pentecost. Then this miracle familiar apostle went on to deny Christ. Peter also opposed Jesus' going to the cross and was harshly rebuked by Him. Jesus told him, "...*for thou knowest (have in mind) not the things that are of God, but the things that are of men.*" Peter was looking at things with the carnal mind; he was determined to fight for Christ in the garden with the "sword of the flesh." And the weakness of his own fleshly mind and strength betrayed him. It was only through a deep broken repentance that Peter was restored to the Lord and was able to be used in the first great outpouring of the Holy Spirit. The powerful Peter finally had a change of mind.

Repentance is about changing your mind, not your actions; actions follow the changing of your mind. You cannot commit sin unless you first have the thought in your mind to commit it. As a man thinks in his heart; SO HE IS! Paul saw himself with the mind of Christ. He believed he was more than a conqueror, joint heir with Christ, the righteousness of God, an ambassador, etc. He was what He chose to believe and turned the Gentile world upside-down.

In this new day of change and kingdom advancement it is important to walk circumspectly; or with watchfulness and awareness of the manner we advance the kingdom of God. We cannot afford to blindly promote practices and doctrines that are an integral part of our "stream" of ministry.

In Christ, every thing we do, believe, and promote MUST be that which has come out of Revelation of the Spirit. Being taught by godly men and women is not the same as revelation of the Spirit. God can use these to impart revelation, but experience and history has shown that even godly men and women have false mindsets concerning the church and its function. We must learn to discern the voice of the Holy Spirit and what is His truth. Much of what is accepted as unquestionable truth in the church has its origin in mans wisdom and works.

TRADITIONS AND MINDSETS

There are traditions and mindsets within cultures that can mask themselves as being the wisdom or mind of Christ when in reality they are simply men's thoughts and deeds. Religious traditions or culture can be mistaken as God's ordained manner of thought and practices, when in fact these are just diverse expressions of creation.

There is a western culture and mindset that is individualistic. There is an eastern culture and mindset that is communal or group focused. Both mindsets are not wrong and have validity when brought into subjection to the Mind of Christ. There is a Greek rationalism that has been the basis for much western thought. There are elements of this thought that are valid, but the rational mind cannot receive the things of God, for they are spiritually discerned and are foolishness to the mind of men. No mindset of men is endued with divine virtue of its own merit.

There is much value in understanding Jewish tradition and philosophy. Scripture was written by Jewish authors, and understanding Jewish culture and mindset is important to understanding the idioms and meaning of events and truths recorded in scripture. But, just as Greek, Roman, Western, Eastern, or Mideast minds cannot spiritually discern without the Spirit; Jewish thought and traditions were completely unable to recognize or comprehend the kingdom of God Jesus preached. The traditions they practiced nullified the Word of God. Their interpretation and application of scripture was foreign to the way Jesus interpreted and applied it. The Torah Regulations were a shadow of things to come; Christ Himself. Yet Christ was the light that cast that shadow. We do not focus and promote the shadow, but the real thing Christ Jesus. We are entering into a kingdom where there is no Jew OR Greek, but Christ is ALL in ALL. It is time to surrender all of our differing mindsets in order to embrace the divine wisdom of God: THE MIND OF CHRIST!!

CHAPTER FIVE
DIVINE PROVISION

A ship's captain fought at the helm all night against a storm. In the dark, guided only by a compass, he faithfully fought through the night to keep the course that would lead him to safe harbor. In the faint predawn light he saw a white foaming mass in front of him that signaled waves breaking on a reef. He quickly changed course so as to avoid what the dark just moments before had hidden. The captain could have rationalized that his eyes were playing tricks on him and there was no danger, but the danger would still be there. All of his faithful work would have been to no avail if he hung his ship up on a reef in the increasing light of day.

In the same manner, many godly men and women have faithfully navigated a stormy night of trials in the world. They have continued to turn their focus to the Lord. But as this new day begins, distance traveled and increasing light necessitates corrections and course changes to avert danger. The reefs of destruction are always there, but we are not responsible for what we cannot see. God will not leave us helpless and without provision to accomplish the work for which He has called us. God's light also shows a way to move forward to safely navigate the stormy waters before us.

As far as money and provision is concerned, the light of this new day is shining on these. We are gaining a greater depth of understanding concerning God's heart of giving and self sacrifice. Yet, even greater understanding is coming.

THE WAYS OF THE WORLD IN THE CHURCH

Paul did not put a price tag on his hit series "Corinthians". There were no copyrights or royalty fees for people to use psalms, hymns, and spiritual songs in early church meetings. In fact, Simon the sorcerer was rebuked for trying to buy the gifts of the Spirit. But now, many things birthed of the Spirit have a price tag. The merchandisers in the temple were not much different than the sellers of spiritual things today. No one seemed to have any qualms about the services provided for a fee in the temple except Jesus. The Pharisees must have been upset at the offense Jesus took to the merchandising practices; upset enough to kill. Surely not everyone selling in the temple had evil intentions; it was simply how they did "Temple worship".

We do "Church" the same today. Today's practice of selling books, cd's, copyrights, and royalties of things given by and for God seems as natural as breathing to much of the church. You may not like to hear this, but it IS going to change. Whether people like it or not it will. The dependency on the worlds system of doing business in the church will not stand.

KINGDOM TRANSITION

While God has used existing avenues of monetary transactions to bless people with truth and anointing, He is always drawing us closer to His perfect will. The next level is going to be hard for many godly people. I include myself in this. This is a New Day with greater understandings of truth. He is always moving in new ways to transform us from glory to glory. The path of the righteous is like the light of dawn; it shines brighter and reveals more.

After Pentecost, we see the Spirit of God motivating the early church to give what they had to those in need, not considering what they had their own. This meant rejecting the way the world operates and sacrificing for the people of God; offering all for the love of the brethren.

Real kingdom change and love caused Paul to lay down his life for people, and remove all obstacles that might possibly bring question and disrepute to the name of Jesus. That is why Paul at times worked with his hands to support himself, not taking money from those he ministered to so as not to have anyone question his motives. Was it wrong to accept support and gifts from God's people? No! But, giving originates in the heart of the giver not the receiver.

RELEASE FROM LAW

The apostles are never recorded as promoting the tithe in any way. They did not have to. People full of the Spirit just gave out of the divine nature within. The apostles would be ridiculous to teach people who gave **all** they had to one another to cut it back 90% to give a tithe. The latter house is greater than the former. The latter has greater love, greater giving, and greater sacrifice. It is greater NOT because you are told to do it, but because you want to do it. There is an even greater freedom in Christ that none of us has experienced fully yet. Let us not put into bondage to law those who the Lord has set free. There is a mindset shift that must take place away from a mindset of bondage to law lingering on many.

There are levels of ruling and reigning in Christ that are about walking with divine authority in the realms of heaven. I am talking about spiritual realities and spheres way beyond the realms of this earth. There is no earthly monetary system in these realms. There are spiritual treasures that are given and received. These are given and received even now in many forms on earth. It is God's will that these heavenly realities are expressed on earth as it is in heaven. God's sons are the gateway of this expression of heaven on earth. This is not done through law; it is done through the expression of the nature of Christ in us.

The greatest heavenly treasure we can obtain is the love and compassion of God expressed in and through us. All else is a clanging gong and clashing cymbal, Noise! Those that walk in love will be entrusted with the treasures of heaven and earth. They do not come to this through Law; they come to it through obedience out of LOVE for God and for our brothers and sisters! Where there is love, there is no law. He who is perfected in love has ALREADY FULFILLED the law. Let us go forward into this perfection of love which is the true riches of heaven, and be careful to not focus on laws. These are clanging gongs and cymbals if they are the focus.

I received this wisdom from the Lord regarding giving, "When the Law of the tithe is removed from the church you will see people give like they did in the early church". It is the teaching of the tithe as a law that has killed the giving spirit in men. Thus we have the saying "The Law kills, but the Spirit Gives life." Placing people under the Law of tithing and making it a duty has removed the truth that ALL we have is God's. Under the tithe, a tenth belonged to God, in the kingdom ALL belongs to God, Time, money, possessions, even life itself. We are now living sacrifices, our life and all that pertains to it is not our own.

The teaching of the need to adhere to law in order to be pleasing to God kills in whatever context it is given. The Pharisaical spirit wants us to focus on law and precepts, the Spirit of Life in Christ Jesus wants to fulfill the law in us as we become by nature law abiding. God's purpose for us is not to make us Law abiding, that is a side benefit. His purpose is to make us like the One who fulfilled all the law and the prophet's. Christ came to make us the fulfillment of the law that we might BE the righteousness of God, not just in position or theory, but in reality. We are called to not even be conscious of Law, but to be the living expression of the Law of the Spirit of Life in Christ Jesus. The Law of the Spirit of Life in Christ affects the manner in which all aspects of the kingdom are established, including money, giving, receiving, and provision.

DIVINE PROVISION THROUGH GIVING

No one tithing in love to God is under condemnation. It's simply time to stop preaching law and obey the Holy Spirit. Focusing on what God once required men to do under law is not wisdom for those who are in Christ. We determine out of love to give as a way of life, not out of compulsion or duty. Paul encouraged the Corinthian Church to set aside a portion on a regular basis as each one determined in their hearts to meet a specific need. This is wonderful truth, and truth that is found in a love relationship with the Lord and with our brothers and sisters. It's time to teach people to hear and obey the voice of the Lord to them in regular and spontaneous giving.

Divine provision should come through the various members of the body. Every joint supplies, there is no lack in Christ. All of this finds its place in love and obedience to the Holy Spirit. For those who depend upon the generosity of others, the removal of the law of the tithe is the kingdom come!! The kind of giving coming will be seen in people laying money at the feet of those with the task of preaching the gospel of the kingdom.

...Freely ye have received, freely give. ~Jesus~

When Jesus spoke these words, He was sending His disciples out to minister healing, deliverance, and proclaim the message of the Kingdom. Let me be clear, teaching on true giving is good, needed, and not wrong. It is important for elders to be the example to others of this. But when it is all said and done it is the sole responsibility of the giver to decide when and how much by direction of the Holy Spirit. The prevailing teaching on giving is receiver promoted. The times are changing.

THE ARTS AND PROVISION

God is opening new avenues for artists and authors to release their works. Not just musicians, but artists will receive their wages in abundance as the Lord of Hosts prepares all the necessary tools, facilities, and distribution capabilities necessary to release His creative power through word, song, and artistry.

A workman will get much more in God's economy than they have received previously by the system of the world. When faith reaches the level of trusting God to supply needs, and not the world's system of promotion, pricing, and profiteering, we will see the industry of Christian music and writing change dramatically. The dependency on the worlds system of doing business in the church will end. Thank God for that! I look forward to the day that the workman is given by those he works for what they decide in their hearts and not what the workman and their handlers decide.

God is going to open new avenues for artists and authors to release their works. Not just musicians, but artists will receive their wages in abundance as the Lord of Hosts prepares all the necessary tools, facilities, and distribution capabilities necessary to release His creative power through word, song, and artistry. But where does it start? Recognizing that what now exists is not our destination. What exists is not where we are going and it is going to change.

MONEYCHANGERS IN THE TEMPLE –
A SHORT STORY OF FICTION

My Name is Lydia. I live in Philippi, Macedonia. I once heard of an apostle named Paul. He was so anointed. We were a small synagogue that was struggling you see. We could not afford a building and were meeting to pray down by the river. One night my husband had a dream and in it he saw Paul. He begged him in the dream to come and help us. He woke up and realized that it was a dream from God and that God was going to let Paul know we needed help. He didn't come, and didn't come. We finally sent off letter to him and waited.

A LETTER FROM PAUL

Years later we at the small synagogue were excited; a letter out of the blue came from Paul saying he was willing now to come to our city. But our excitement waned as we read on. He said he would have come earlier but he had a minimum requirement of 1000 denarius per meeting. He knew we were small and couldn't afford him at the time, so he didn't bother coming the first time. But he was sure by now we had saved enough money, and could advertise his arrival to all the synagogues in the surrounding areas. We had no money. We were crushed.

But not to worry, he had now written some books! Well, we couldn't afford those either, the two volume Corinthian series was 35 denarius a book, but on special 55 denarius for both. He wrote he could come and pray for us for a donation! But the cost of breaking off generational curses was a donation minimum of 100 denarius per session, per person. We would have to live with our curses. But wait, we had hope! If we want to be in relationship with Him, we only have to sign a covenant agreement with him to be part of his network. But the only way we can have relationship with him is to agree to pay a monthly fee or give a percentage of all money we are supposed to collect from our poverty stricken congregation. We didn't have enough money to be his friend either.

It said in the letter we can get his worship leader to come! But we have to rent a coliseum and charge 15 denarius a head. We can't afford the coliseum, so we can't afford to worship God.

We then read he's holding a conference on how to prosper in the 1rst century apostolic movement, but it will cost 75 denarius for pre-registration, or 100 at the door.

We decided to sign up for his newsletter. This newsletter would give us the latest revelations and insights into what God is doing in the 1rst century. But when we received the newsletter it was a three paragraph teaser ad for buying his latest book, and the rest was full of ads for books he was selling by other apostles and prophets. Once again, we could not afford to hear from God and get the help we needed. We were crestfallen. Well anyway, I once heard of an apostle named Paul.

CHAPTER SIX
JEZEBEL AND ELIJAH

Jezebel! What is this behemoth power that seemingly rises from the very pit of hell itself? It has brought great ministers and ministries to the dust. It has hindered and opposed the work and will of God on the earth. It has usurped, undermined, and perverted the God given authority to men, women, churches, and movements intended to shake the very foundations of the earth. It has crumbled nations and dethroned kings and queens.

Reach over across your body and shake your opposite hand (if you have one). Let me introduce you to the source from which this power called Jezebel has the potential to rise. It is the uncrucified flesh of men exerting it's will into the affairs of God and man. The Jezebel that dominates most of the church today is not sourced in a demonic spirit; it is sourced in the fleshly desires of men for the pleasing of self. The people who are afflicted with a "spirit" of Jezebel have (these are my terms) "a spiritual condition like that of Jezebel" spoken of in I Kings and Revelations 2:20-23.

THE JEZEBEL JESUS JUDGES
Notwithstanding I have a few things against thee because thou sufferest that woman Jezebel (who calls herself a prophetess) to teach and to seduce my servants to commit fornication, and to eat things sacrificed unto idols.   And I have given her time to repent of her fornication, and she repented not. ~Jesus~

Many consider Jezebel to be a spirit. But, the Jezebel Jesus confronts is not a spirit. Jesus did not say, "You have a Jezebel spirit in your midst." He is giving a **person** time to **repent** because they are leading God's children astray like the Jezebel of Elijah's

79

day. I have been attacked demonically when dealing with Jezebel. Any time you mess with people's uncrucified flesh there are demonic forces surrounding wickedness that keep the person bound and assist in propagating wickedness.

If you think you can just confront a spirit and Jezebel will go away you are wrong. You have only dealt with part of the problem. The cross and repentance is the answer for stinking flesh. That is why Jesus gives her time to repent, and doesn't tell the people of Thyatira to "cast out the devil Jezebel". Repentance is the key to shut the open door Jezebel has swung wide to devils. Intolerance of her sin is the only way to root her out. She must repent or leave. If she refuses to repent and is the "leader", then those who are righteous must leave. When you tolerate Jezebel (regardless of the position or title) your spiritual discernment becomes dull. Jezebel is NOT a women thing; both men and women exhibit this behavior.

Jezebel is all about positions of power and authority. Many places of authority in the church are held by Jezebel. Many people in places of authority in the church are influenced and controlled by a Jezebel with no position of authority themselves. Jezebel may practice any fleshly or demonic method to advance their position of authority, or access and usurp another's position of authority. Here is a list of methods used by people who are Jezebel. These methods are practiced by established leadership as well as those who are trying to exert their will over others in places of authority.

Flattery- Flattery attempts to inject pride into people that puffs up their flesh and prepares them to receive the demands of their flesh as legitimate God given rights. It is the way in which a person who walks in the likeness of Jezebel brings others to join them on their journey of Spiritless endeavors promoting works of the flesh in the name of God.

Seduction- This involves compromise that takes people one small step at a time until before they know it they are no longer where they once were. Before long they have deceived themselves into thinking they are doing God's will. This method can literally lead to fornication and adultery in some cases. But it leads to spiritual adultery in all cases.

Lying- This weapon is used to impress people with fictional exploits or promises. It is used also to defame and discredit those who are walking in the true anointing, authority, and power of God. Many times it can work its magic also by causing bitterness in the one being attacked, causing much damage.

Intimidation- Like the Jezebel of old who used intimidation on Elijah; this has the potential to literally shut down the anointing of those who will let fear rule over them.

Controlling and Manipulating –This is how Jezebel keeps people in line and following even when they have lost all desire to do so. Fear of being in disobedience to God or being in rebellion to God is a great motivator that Jezebel uses to keep her flock intact and in line.

Great Piety and Holiness (set apartness) – Jezebel humbly makes it known the great service they have done, how much they pray, and the great spiritual gifts, revelation, and impartation they have received from God. This can involve some sort of special spiritual insight, power, or impartation they have that people must receive from them alone. Such as; deliverance, fullness, the Seven-fold Spirit of God, etc. It is used to prey on the immature and to try to impress the mature.

There are probably more, but these are some tools of Jezebel I have encountered. I have even used some of these in my stints as Jezebel. Yes! Jezebel is ME uncrucified. It is self exerting its will in the affairs of God and man.

DEMISE OF THE EARLY CHURCH

After Jesus ascends and the Spirit is poured out, it doesn't take long before we see people start to follow the world's way of doing things. In Rev. 2:6 Jesus deplores the deeds and doctrines of the Nicolaitans. The word Nicolaitans means to "subdue, conquer, or be victorious over the people."

After the first apostles were dead, and those that knew them also had passed away, the Nicolaitan way had finally won out in the western church. The final blow came with Constantine's flesh advanced church, and the raising up of the Church of Rome and its leader as the seat of all power in the church. A system mimicking the world was established with a king (pope), regional governors (arch bishops), city rulers (bishops) and tax collectors (priests/pastors).

Jezebel (the flesh driven will of men) now had established **systemic false authority** in the church. In the Roman church, men had to pay for forgiveness, blessing, and even the licenses to commit sin. No more did the people have a voice in the church, but the Pope's word was law. God became inaccessible to the common man apart from going through the priest. Men became completely dependant upon the church for any spiritual life at all. Jezebel loves to have people dependant upon her.

BIRTHING OF NEW THINGS

During the reformation, a stirring of the Holy Spirit brings life to those willing to accept truth outside of the precepts of the Church. The reformation restored truths to the people that gave them a faith for salvation that was not dependant upon a man. Luther's revelation was the first drops of rain in a flood of change that was about to come. Though much has changed, in structure the church groups that emerged and still are emerging remain much like their mother, the Church of Rome. Much was lost over the Dark Ages. The slave like mindset of needing a human leader is set as doctrinal certainty in most of her children. The making of church as a place to go to instead of being the "people", made the "place" sacred and the people only as sacred as their faithfulness to come to that place.

OVERCOMING JEZEBEL

In the early to mid 1990's there was a wave of refreshing God brought to those willing to receive it. This was God's grace to the church and His mercy to Jezebel. In effect, this marked the beginning of a time period He was giving her to repent and walk in freedom. In many places, we saw Jezebel (the flesh of men) strengthen her grip on power. Much of the fruit of this refreshing was devoured by leadership taking advantage of this movement to further their own positions and interests. What was meant to empower people was stifled by an entrenched hierarchal system.

There was also an unction poured out during that refreshing that fell upon many. This was a prophetic anointing sent to deal with Jezebel and bring the church transition and restoration. Many who received this unction began prophesying the things on God's heart. But as prophecy does, the words began to bring persecution and rejection by Jezebel and those in her grip. Some compromised and became like Balaam, pleasing men for money. They became prophets of Jezebel.

Like in Elijah's day, many of the "prophets" were shunned or driven out of the churches by Jezebel. Some were called out by the Lord. Some started their own churches; some becoming the very thing they had prophesied against. Some wallowed in bitterness and began prophesying destruction. These bitter voices have been slowly decreasing as God has not blessed their bitterness with progressive revelation. But, many like Elijah have learned to walk with God in the wilderness. Hidden in drying up brooks, they have faced times of great failure and humiliation stemming from their own flesh. But in the midst of the wilderness they have changed. They have become dependant upon God for their needs.

A LACK OF RAIN

Jezebel and Elijah have both experienced the lack of rain. Jezebel has had nothing of substance to offer people and they have begun to leave the barren wasteland of "church" by the thousands. Elijah also has experienced this lack, but has found sustenance from the very hand of God. God has gently fed and disciplined Elijah. Elijah has realized he becomes Jezebel if he follows his own flesh and has learned he must put it to death.

Those hidden in the wilderness are coming back. They went out frustrated and angry. They are coming back in peace and rest. They will not tolerate Jezebel or the false perverted Nicolaitan teachings that subject God's people as slaves to the will of other men. The grace and beauty of mature children following their Father, not men, will once again bring the outpouring of the Holy Spirit that will eclipse the days of the Acts of the Apostles. These hidden ones also bring with them Fire and Rain.

FIRE

These coming carry the fire of God's presence. This fire is a witness that God is with them. This fire will stir the passion of God's love in people for God, and for each other. Jezebel and her prophets do not have this fire, and are incapable of manifesting a love originating from the presence of God. The name Jezebel can mean one who is an "Island" or "not dwelt with". Flesh (Jezebel) is incapable of intimate, true fellowship with God or man. Jezebel's manner of existing in the church is based upon position, power, and mans approval; not true eye to eye relationships.

The fire coming will also bring cleansing and repentance to many. The fire of judgment will consume many who refuse to repent and allow God to change them. This will be the point at which Jezebel's time has run out. Those embodying her likeness will either repent or slip into darkness as God will turn them over to their enemies to be afflicted.

RAIN

From God's presence is coming a wave of refreshing. The rain will pour as Elijah begins to restore all things. Restoration of relationships, healing, and blessing will flow freely from the presence of the Lord. The streams of Living water from these rains will flow, and those parched with thirst will be refreshed and restored. These will join in the labor of turning the desert wasteland into a fruitful field.

RESTORATION

The body will have its authority restored. The one thing Jezebel coveted and stripped from the people of God was their places of authority. A renewed sense of purpose and destiny will invigorate the church as dead dreams and visions will come back to life. Abandoned mantles will fall again upon many. As this restoration brings about true love and humility, it will be hard for Jezebel to find a place among the true church. Positions and titles will be of little consideration. The true church will simply not tolerate her anymore. The old church system of leadership from the top down will eventually be discarded and forgotten like a filthy rag. Those with true spiritual authority within a congregation will begin to refuse titles, and serve alongside their brothers and sisters. Their preoccupation will be enabling others to minister. Those that overcome Jezebel will walk in the true kingdom authority.

CHAPTER SEVEN
WHAT IS TO COME

I believe it is of the Lord what I am going to share. It is important to understand what is to come in order to put our focus where it should be when it happens, ON HIM, and the unfolding of His presence and power WITHIN His people. While catastrophic events and great fear will grip the earth, those who are in Him will not be shaken.

The Lord is coming to purify and cleanse His bride. Judgment **must come first to His house**, and then to all of creation. In the process of doing this He must shake things that affect all of creation in order to free her from the grip of the world's systems. He has brought the systems of men down before, and for the sake of His bride He will do it again for good. God loves all of mankind; so much so He sent Jesus Christ to die. Man-made institutions are just systems not men. Systems are ways in which people interact and divide themselves. It is important to not be hoping in a system, be it based upon economic, political, religious, or military form of stability. God is determined to deliver creation from the sin of pride and self centeredness. But, when these which are the building blocks of Babylon are nullified and Babylon falls; those who hope in her will fall. This may take many years to unfold, but the Kingdom of God is going to be established in the midst of great tribulation; resulting in the rising and falling of many.

The Lord has made it clear to me that much of the trouble (tribulation) that is coming is first for God's cleansing of His people, and then for the sake of His people becoming overcomers. Some of the tribulation will be the strong reaction of the enemy to the Brides unveiling. There will also be tribulation as the result of the Bride passing judgment on sin. This will be done with all grace and ample opportunity for repentance in order that all who call on the Name of the Lord will be saved.

The Kingdom Age will envelope every aspect of life until we will no longer say "know the Lord" as everyone who remains in this age of the Kingdom after completed purging will know Him from the least to greatest. The Kingdom of God has had a limited effect on man made institutions as men in them have individually yielded to Him. But, we will see man made institutions crumble and turn to dust as the rock uncut by hands grows into the mountain of the Lord.

REGIONAL KINGDOM MANIFESTATION

"...when the most High caused the Gentiles to be inherited, when he separated the sons of men, he set the bounds of the peoples according to the number of the sons of Israel." ~Moses~

Moses is clearly stating in this verse that God has divided the earth's boundaries into regions. These regions are according to the number of the sons of Israel; (Jacob) twelve tribes in all. There will be twelve distinct regions of divine influence across the globe with varying expressions of the Lord's favor for each one. These expressions are manifesting in the natural twelve particular spiritual expressions in the realms of heaven. These expressions are represented by the twelve stones of the "breastplate of judgment" on the priest's Ephod (from Exodus 28), as well as the twelve types of precious stones that make up the foundation of the New Jerusalem.

These regions, or expressions of the kingdom, are not governed by law, but by the presence of God's throne in the midst of His people. These specific regions on the earth serve as a resting place of His glory and presence. "Heaven on earth" This is a result of his people manifesting His glory through what they have become; resting places of His glory, the manifestation of Christ in man. As individuals find their place in Him, and also become a resting place for Him, there will be freedom and deliverance from the works of the devil.

The Lord's purpose is to see His kingdom come on earth as it is in heaven, as a result of His people living out and expressing spiritual realities on earth as it is in heaven. As the days go on and troubles increase these places of refuge will be sought out for their distinct expressions of the manifest presence of God according to need. You will also see people refusing to repent flee these places for regions that are under the domain of the devil for a season. You will also see refugees flee to the regions of God's presence from the regions of lawlessness.

The foundation of the rule of God in these regions will not be the power sources of men's ruling today. The seat of God's power is His corporate bride unveiled and descending from heaven. These places of kingdom reign are not built on laws, politics, economic prosperity, or military power; but on righteousness, joy, and peace in the Holy Spirit. Righteousness and justice will be the foundation of God's rule over these regions. God will rule through His people, executing judgments and the decrees of heaven through their mouths.

In the regions of "The peace of God's presence", there will be greater and greater manifestations of God's Glory as sickness and poverty will be wiped out. The economy of Love that gives what you have to those in need and consider nothing as your own like the early church, will replace the monetary system of Babylon. A system of serving and loving will supply everyone's needs. Food and shelter will be provided as those who have will supply for those who don't, and the cycle will go on and on. The land and weather patterns of these regions will be blessed. This is only possible with the rule of law being removed, and the Law of the Spirit of Life taking over as the kingdom advances.

DISINTEGRATION OF THE RULE OF LAW

As the seat of God's kingdom the New Jerusalem/The Corporate Bride emerges, we will see in the world simultaneously the progressive disintegration of governments and rule of law among men. The places of safety and security in the governments of men will wither away and become ineffective to stop lawlessness from taking control of whole regions. This disintegration must happen as the kingdom that is being established is not founded upon anything that current governments are founded upon. This must happen in order for the Kingdom to fully be established.

National boundaries will blur and power will be to armed groups that will be in control and not central or local governments. These regions will be in great darkness, and men will be given over to all sorts of unspeakable acts that will make Hitler and Stalin look mild compared to the "sport" that men will make with the lives of other men. In the same way God manifests in His people, so the devil will manifest his nature and deeds through his servants. They will terrorize and lay waste to even the land.

We are about to see the maturing and harvest of ALL things, both good and evil. There will be a clear separating of the wheat and the tares; the sons of God and the sons of the devil. The choice of trusting or not trusting in God will be clear for all to see, all creation will be made cognizant of this division in both heaven and earth and under the earth, there will be no excuses for any man, woman, child, or angelic being; as it will be made clear unto all. And yet even with great turmoil and trouble, many men will continue in their ways and delusions because they have given themselves over to wickedness. They will have no excuse on that day of His appearing; as He will have made known through His people His great and glorious goodness and mercy. His manifold wisdom will be on display for all to see, even to the whole of creation, through His Bride, the church, the called out ones.

Let both grow together until the harvest, and in the time of harvest I will say to the reapers, Gather ye together first the tares and bind them in bundles to burn them, but gather the wheat into my barn.

The maturing of God's children into His likeness is going to be seen as the holiness of God will be manifest on the earth through His people. God is coming into union with His people and He is revealing Himself and His nature through His son's. He is uniting himself with His people as a groom unites Himself with His bride, bone of her bone and flesh of her flesh. The two are becoming one.

The maturing of evil is also upon us as well, as man's inhumanity to men will be seen as never before. The devil is coming into union with his chosen, who are about to express the fullness of his nature; a murderer and liar. They will truly be seen for what they are; sons of their father the devil. Great darkness covers and will cover the earth, but as darkness increases the light will shine brighter and brighter.

"...the field is the world; the good seed are the sons of the kingdom, but the tares are the sons of the wicked; and the enemy that sowed them is the devil; the harvest is the end of the age, and the reapers are the angels. As therefore the tares are gathered and burned in the fire, so shall it be in the end of this age." ~Jesus~

Eventually all that offends will be rooted out and burned. The harvest of the righteous will be all that remains, but for this time before us we can expect to see upheaval and stress never seen before on the earth. This is the separation and polarization that takes place now at the end of the age (which is now over). We have entered a "New Day" as it were and now we are going to see this happen. There will be an expression of the fullness of Christ and His love in His people as they lay down their lives (truly martyred in preaching to and loving the lost) to save as many of the sons of men as are willing to repent. Those expressing the murder and lies of the devil will meet "unquenchable fire".

"...whose fan is in his hand; and he will thoroughly purge his threshing floor and gather his wheat into the storehouse, but he will burn up the chaff with fire that shall never be quenched" ~John the Baptist~

THE PLACE OF GOD'S THRONE

There is an errant replacement theology that says "Israel" is now those born of the Spirit and the natural Israel is no longer eligible for the promises of God. God is going to fulfill every promise to the Jewish people He made in Scripture. But, He is fulfilling all the promises from a heavenly perspective as well. Her restoration to God will truly mean the complete resurrection of the dead in Christ.

Throughout history, when the Jews have been in rebellion against God the nations around them are stirred up by Him to trouble Israel. We are in the time of troubling and strife of men that will cause the Jews in rebellion to their Messiah to cry out to God. This is the day of Jacob's trouble (tribulation). God is chastising the Jewish people with the pressure of being pressed on every side. This serves the purpose of bringing Israel back as an unfaithful wife to her husband. At the same time the gentile church through much "tribulation" will enter the kingdom of God. God is after hearts, men are focused on land. The land will come after the hearts are purified.

Those Jews in the land of Israel are going to have no hope of survival in the natural. This is so that her rescue may be from God, not from their might or the might of another nation. Then when she cries out she will be delivered. She has been brought back to her land after 2000 years, and is positioned now to play the role she was destined to play, bringing life from the dead through her reconciliation. One day God's Jewish people will ask their enemies to dwell with them in peace and share their land because their hearts will be that of Christ.

As the earth enters the day of His appearing, we will see both the spiritual and physical cities coming into union. He is bringing those of Israel in the natural and spiritual into completion together. The natural Israel will embrace their Messiah and unite with the spiritual. The reign of God will fully be manifesting though His people which have become not only "One New Man" with their Jewish brothers and sisters; but "One New City" of peace in which God's Throne is set with men. As the New Jerusalem descends from Heaven, and is unveiled; the "Son of David" will reign in the hearts of men, and then on the earth. The spiritual dwelling of the New Jerusalem is even now in the process of descending, or being unveiled as a bride to receive fully her groom. Jerusalem both physically and spiritually will be the place of His throne, and the ruling seat of the Kingdom of God on earth.

THE CHURCH (EKKLESIA) CALLED OUT ONES

The word church (Ekklesia) means "called out". The word "Saints" which also describes the church means "to be holy or separated unto God." It's important to understand what the Ekklesia (church) has been called out (separated) unto. We are not called out to a new system, new denomination, new network style, or new church structure. Men have built these institutions for centuries and have failed to produce the fullness of God's kingdom.

Jesus said "I will build (form the structure of) my church." We are called out of Babylon to manifest the portion of His being He forms in us. He makes the connections and networks us with other people according to His specifications. He does this connecting through people whose function is to connect people. But He does this in a way that gives expression to His nature; taking focus off structure and putting it on the most important thing; the presence and dwelling of God IN men.

God is expressing His nature and authority through people in ways that are not boxed and packaged by men's systems. Men are trying to build a structure, a network, a system of church; in effect a tower of Babel; expecting that the Word of the Lord and the gifts will make what they've built an acceptable offering to the Lord. The Lord is calling out those who will gather unto Him, and order themselves in the manner in which He forms His church. When we gather unto Him in His formation; He is expressed fully through His people.

The church is not an organizational structure as much an expression, each individual a unique expression of the person of Jesus Christ. God is more interested in seeing Christ (His identity) formed in each person than an organizational structure. The structure He is building is the fullness of the measure of the stature of Christ, His body, His dwelling, His fully united "one flesh" Bride. When we stop DOING church and start BEING the church; the glory of God will be revealed to His people, and then through them to all of creation.

SHOWING THE UNIVERSE HIS WISDOM

Being His bride fulfills our destiny and the purpose for which we were called out. That purpose is that through the church His manifold wisdom will be seen by all creation, including principalities and powers in heavenly places and the entire universe. My earthly father used to preach, "That we would even dispossess the malignant principalities and powers". We wrestle against principalities and powers because we are wrestling away their places of power that we might occupy those places.

What a high calling we have, and what and inheritance we have in Christ, and what a love that Father has poured on us to bring us into conformity to His image as His children. Truly we are His inheritance and He is our inheritance as we become one with Christ in purpose, in nature, and authority. All of creation groans for this expression of Christ in God's sons.

THE BEGINNING

In this new day Babylon (the world's system) is falling. She falls to great destruction. Babylon has the blood of the saints and prophets in her. As the systems of men fall and all of its trades sink in the sea with flames, a new order rises. In the end the Kingdom of God will be established; whose security is not the might of men, his political structures, his wisdom, or financial resources.

When Scripture refers to the last days it is referring to the last days of the world under the control of men's flesh. The doorway for Satan to reign on the earth has been the self-serving flesh of men building edifices of power and glory unto their own names. The last days of sin are ending, and the beginning days of the reign of righteousness, joy, and peace in the Holy Spirit are here.

It is not a time for fear, but a time for faith. It is not a time to focus on saving the worlds systems which are shaking, but to establish the kingdom that cannot be shaken. It is the very establishing of the kingdom of God that is bringing the shaking. It is the beginning of the earth and heavens being purified and cleansed for an eternity of God's presence, passion, and oneness with His creation.

ADDENDUM

FOUR HORNS OF ZECHARIAH CHAPTER ONE

<u>**MILITARY POWER (WORKS OF THE FLESH)**</u> – Exerting influence over others through dominance, control, coercion, extortion, military might, intimidation, threats, and bullying, etc

<u>**POLITICAL POWER**</u> – Influences on the formation and administration of institutions by various interest groups with self serving agendas. This is achieved through legitimate or illegitimate power structures within the institution. These political interests groups may have a power base from ethnic, cultural, issue related groups, religious groups, etc.

<u>**RELIGIOUS POWER**</u> – Theologies, philosophies, ideologies, doctrines, traditions, religious regulations or worldviews that unite, motivate, and empower groups to exert power through political, military, or economic means.

<u>**ECONOMIC POWER**</u> - Money and/or its representative physical resources or possessions. Money is translated to power as it can purchase influence; influence that can enable religious power and purchase political and military power.

PICTURES OF WHAT THE "CHURCH" IS

The church is a family. We are made in the image of God our Father. Jesus said "I will build my church". Scripture gives us various pictures as to what it is that He is building. These symbolic pictures of the church give us clarity as to what the church is and the purpose of God for building it.

The Temple Of God The church is a temple (building), the dwelling place of God. The purpose of the temple is to become a place God may rest or ABIDE. As Living stones, His people have become the abiding or resting place of the Holy Spirit corporately and individually. It is in this place that worshippers find and commune with their God; Jesus said, "Those who worship God will worship Him in spirit (the inner man) and in truth." It is no more a focus on external gathering places and gathering procedures, but now we are fitted together (connected) spiritually; each of us with a unique function and place, and God is both WITH and IN us, not "out there" somewhere.

The Body Of Christ A body expresses the will of the mind/head. While all body parts have different functions, they are all connected to the brain and have one purpose, to do the will of the brain. The "mind" or brain being in charge is a must, as following some other impulse is a sign of dysfunction. It is a natural thing for an arm to move when the brain commands it to move. Some organs are on automatic from the "head" but ALL organs function only as the nerves are connected to and under the control of the head.

In the same manner, Christ's body is formed to express the divine nature and will of God. As His body, we are indeed **PART/Partakers** of His divine nature, and are indeed expression of the person of Jesus Christ. Having the "mind" of Christ means we each respond to and act according to the thoughts and impulses of the Holy Spirit, and not acting on other impulses that implicate dysfunction. We are inseparable and all are part of **ONE** organism made up of many smaller parts. **ONENESS** or interdependent connectedness with each other is also the implication of God's purpose for the body. We recognize that there is one body with one purpose, one goal, one covenant, and one head.

The Bride Of Christ While all these previous descriptions are true about the church, Scripture culminates in the Revelation of John with a picture of the Bride of Christ (the church) as the New Jerusalem, the holy city and dwelling place of God prepared by God to have eternal union with the Son. A city represents a plurality or multitude of people which the Father has chosen to come into UNION with the Lamb, and in doing so Himself.

In John's revelation the Bride has made herself ready, and has been prepared by God for an intimate consummating relationship of union with The Lamb. After 2000 years of struggle strife, and pain, we are at the door of this consummating relationship, as the bride is about to come into the fullness of the purpose for which she was called out and set apart for; Becoming ONE with God.

COMING UP FROM THE WILDERNESS

By Kriston Couchey

You go down thinking you came to get equipped
You come up knowing you just got stripped
You go down awed at those who claim to know God but just don't get it
You come up awed at how you claimed to know God and just didn't get it
You go down thinking you are the least of the apostles
You come out knowing you are the chief of sinners
You go down confident you are God's man for the job
You come up with no confidence at all in yourself
You go down saying, "I am different, and it will not take me long."
You come up saying "I thought it would never end!"
You go down angry with those who rejected you and the gift on your life
You come up offering your life so that those same people are not destroyed
You go down thinking you are searching for God
You come up knowing He was seeking you
You go down preoccupied with the purity of doctrine
You come up preoccupied with the purity of holiness
You go down relishing the day you will prophesy like Elijah
You come up like Moses, convinced you are not qualified for the task
You go down fantasizing about the great wonders you will do
You come up preferring solitude with peace and quietness
You go down a praying man who knows what words to pray
You come up having lost the meaning of words since you learned to be silent before Him
You go down concerned about the matters of life and ministry
You come up knowing nothing matters but Him
You go down speaking, proclaiming, and calling forth your destiny
You come up grateful if you get to be a doorkeeper in the outer court
You go down always having the last word for those who oppose you
You come up unable to say anything except what you hear your Father say
You go down looking for the promised land of rest
You come up knowing you finally found it in Him
You go down seeking miracles, power and ministry
You come up lost in Love, leaning upon your Beloved

NOW YOU WILL SHAKE

Kriston Couchey

Now you will shake, let the Praises begin

Now you will shake, As My Glory comes in

As it is in the Spirit, So it's witnessed on earth

Now you will shake, As the Spirit gives birth

Transitional Labor, Is painful and strong

No more intermissions, The contractions are long,

Now will shake, Let My Glory arise

Even though you have heard it, The truth will surprise

My Glory brings judgment, Both sorrow and peace

For some separation, For others release

I'm accepting an offering, First fruits unto Me

A number in millions, Devoted and free

Now you will shake, Do not fear what you see

Now you will shake, Keep your focus on Me

ABOMINATION THAT MAKES DESOLATE

By Kriston Couchey

Is my temple made with human hands?
Are not My people the dwelling place of My Spirit and Glory?
Who has taken up residence in the house of My Glory?
Is it not the "God" of your own making?
Is this false Christ (antichrist) you worship not formed after your own
image and not Mine?
Yet you call this Christ by my name, "Jesus"?
A stench rises from My temple.
Your "Jesus" is self exalting and rewards those who lord over their
brothers.
This "Christ" does not drive out the abomination of thieves making
merchandise of my people.
He honors the sons of Eli, exalting those who seize the best portions
for themselves.
He winks at those who satisfy their lustful desires upon the vulnerable
among my people.
Shall I keep silent about this abomination?
Shall I bless those who worship this idol of self?
As in the days of Eli; My Glory is departed and you are given over to
your enemies in desolation.
But, those who minister before me like Samuel shall be blessed and
their words shall not fall to the ground.
They shall inherit the places of those made desolate and herald the
coming King.

MIDDLE EAST RELIGIOUS FUNDAMENTALISM

By Kriston Couchey

Those religious men, so hateful toward all that I love,
Looking for blood, ready to slay that which defies their religious
traditions,

Secret counsels in the dark,
They hiss, "This freedom is a threat to our way of life, we must stop
it!"

In secrecy they come, in the dark,
I swore to Him, now I will not let Him down,

Sweaty palms grip the hilt of a garment-hidden sword,
They approach with torches and sword,

Bravely I stand for righteousness,
How dare they attack such nobility and grace, my very Lord!

I pull out my sword and lunge at the evil men,
Yes! A blow struck for goodness and truth,

But wait, My Lord? Why do you rebuke me so harshly?
Almost as harshly as the time I said, "You will not go to the cross!"

Why do you heal this wicked mans ear?
I fling my strength and confidence into the darkness with my sword,

I am ashamed; my Master willingly is led like a sheep to the slaughter!

I'M MORE THAN AN APOSTLE

Kriston Couchey

I'm more than an apostle, and if there's any doubt,
Let me tell the story how this mystery came about,

The men they called apostles, were always at the top,
They preached and prayed for hours, pushing people till they
dropped.

I naturally decided, this life it was for me,
My future was the brightest, fame and popularity

Apostles got the most respect, a following of men,
No matter what their needs might be, a servant would attend,

A woman in a wedding gown kept swooning at their side,
They indulged in making love to her and didn't try to hide,

No one seemed to notice, so I thought I'd get some too,
But while I was in passion with the bride, in walked the groom,

We covered up our nakedness; tears were on His face,
But every word He spoke to her was full of love and grace,

He said "My dear you're lovely", placed his hands upon her hips,
He wiped a shameful tear away and kissed her on the lips.

And slowly now he turned to me and looked me in the eye,
I realized that this might be the day I finally die,

He said, "Attend us servant, and wash my ladies feet,

Then wash her dress and mend it, and bring us food to eat,"

"But before you start your service, a eunuch you must be,
The cutting will be painful, but this bride belongs to me."

My urge to be apostle, was finally in doubt,
No one ever told me what their work was all about.

He said "There is an option; the choice is up to you."
And then he broke into a smile, that made me smile too,

I'm more than an apostle, and if you think I've lied,
I'm more than an apostle, for He chose me for His bride

LAYING DOWN YOUR LIFE FOR THE SHEEP

Kriston Couchey

The true heart of the apostolic and prophetic office
It is interesting the debate going on over titles these days. Personally I don't pay any attention to anyone's title. I look at how they function and how much of the Lord I see in them.

I am not impressed with teachings.
I am not impressed with titles.
I am not impressed with men's' approval.
I am not impressed with someone's anointing.
I am not impressed with someone's dream or vision.
I am not impressed with words of knowledge, they are a tool.
I am not impressed with healings. God is the healer anyway.
I am not impressed with size of ministry.
I am not impressed with someone's sphere of influence.

What impresses me?
Paul Said "Death is at work in me that life may be at work in you."
I am impressed with someone broken over the condition of God's people.
I am impressed with someone who is more concerned about seeing the people of God function in THEIR gifts, than having to administer his own.
I am impressed when a "leader" can take correction from ANYONE! Even the world.
I am impressed when I see someone gently deal with immaturity and not destroy a person over a dumb mistake.
I am impressed when a person sees potential in people rather than just the failures.

I am impressed when I see someone who doesn't just make friends with their own "leadership" peers, or those who can forward their ministry. But they associate with those who are problem people and considered hopeless causes.

I am impressed with someone who will go through a whole meeting not having to preach or teach, but rest in their authority in the realm of the spirit and just be a watchman, letting God be God through and to His people.

I am impressed with a person who trusts God enough to trust His people.

I am impressed by those who I will never know, who in the secret place of prayer gave and sacrificed in prayer and fasting for the life of another.

I am impressed with someone so broken and humble they prefer to not draw attention to themselves or their own teachings, but let others be first.

I am impressed when I see the character of God in someone.

I am impressed when I see someone lay down their life for the sheep.

TO YOU I HAVE COME MY BELOVED

Kriston Couchey

To You I have come My Beloved,
The day of our union is here,
A day for which long I have waited,
The fruit of loves passion appears,

Desire it burns deep within me,
Jealousy spurring me on,
What stands in loves way will fear me,
For you are to be wholly mine

You medicate wounds with your lovers
You love them as you should love me
Their medicines they cannot heal you
My undying love sets you free,

So open your arms to embrace me,
And turn from the darkness of night,
I take you to heights of my passion,
I clothe you in garments of white

The groom and the bride they are wedding,
Let those come against us who may
My fervor of love will not falter
I've come and will wed you this day

WORDS OF WISDOM

I regret the times God sent me with the sword of truth to cut loose the chains of a bound man, and I returned to present Him their severed head.

This (religious) system has furthered the positions and power of the few, while enslaving the many. Let's say it in love, "God hates it!" He does not hate the people in the system. He hates that which has aborted, defiled, enslaved and deceived His children. And so would you if your children were destroyed by something.

An apostle led church is an apostle led church. A pastor led church is a pastor led church. A Spirit led church is a Spirit led church.

Where did Moses, Elijah, John, and Jesus receive their authority? In the back side of the desert... in the place of quietness and rest....brokenness and weakness. Many want to expose the sin and error of others. But, they never experienced being broken, weak, and emptied in the desert in order to receive authority to confront error and wickedness, like Moses, Elijah, John or Jesus.

~Kriston Couchey~

CPSIA information can be obtained at www.ICGtesting.com
Printed in the USA
BVOW030259290312

286246BV00004B/13/P